PROPAGATING
YOUR PLANTS

PROPAGATING YOUR PLANTS

SOWING SEED, TAKING CUTTINGS, DIVIDING, LAYERING AND
GRAFTING, SHOWN IN 540 PHOTOGRAPHS AND ILLUSTRATIONS

RICHARD ROSENFELD

PHOTOGRAPHY BY PETER ANDERSON

southwater

This edition is published by
Southwater
an imprint of Anness Publishing Ltd
Blaby Road, Wigston
Leicestershire LE18 4SE
info@anness.com

www.southwaterbooks.com
www.annesspublishing.com

If you like the images in this book
and would like to investigate using
them for publishing, promotions or
advertising, please visit our website
www.practicalpictures.com for
more information.

Publisher: Joanna Lorenz
Senior Editor: Felicity Forster
Photography Manager:
    Andrew Mikolajski
Photography: Peter Anderson
Illustrator: Liz Pepperell
Designer: Nigel Partridge
Cover Design: Jonathan Davison
Production Controller: Ben Worley

© Anness Publishing Ltd 2012

A CIP catalogue record for this book
is available from the British Library.

Previously published as part of a
larger volume, *The Gardener's Guide
to Propagation*

PUBLISHER'S NOTES
Although the advice and information
in this book are believed to be
accurate and true at the time of
going to press, neither the authors
nor the publisher can accept any
legal responsibility or liability for
any errors or omissions that may
have been made, nor for any loss,
harm or injury that comes about
from following instructions in
this book.

Great care should be taken if you
decide to include pools, ponds or
water features as part of your garden
landscape. Young children should
never be left unsupervised near water
of any depth, and if children are able
to access the garden all pools and
ponds should be fenced and gated
to the recommended specifications.

In the United States, throughout
the Sun Belt states, from Florida,
across the Gulf Coast, southern
Texas, southern deserts to southern
California and the coastal regions,
annuals are planted in the autumn,
bloom in the winter and spring, and
die at the beginning of summer.

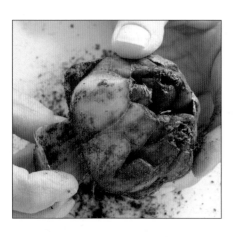

Contents

Introduction

When you are new to gardening, propagation might sound highly specialized, but it is exactly what you do every time you sow lettuces and chilli peppers, marigolds and nasturtiums. Anyone can do it. It is the art of creating more through a natural process. But, like everything else in gardening, you need expert tips on what to do and when, what works and what does not.

Benefits of propagation

Propagating is useful because it will save you a fortune, will help you create larger numbers of plants and, best of all, lets you see nature at work in close up. Once a garden is in full swing, it is a good idea to keep propagating for three very important reasons. First, propagating fills unexpected gaps – and even in the best-planned garden these will occur, often around newly bought plants which have not yet reached their full size. Second, propagating provides replacements for mature plants that are getting tired and ragged, and no longer produce a particularly attractive flower display. Third, it allows you to grow a wide range of annual crops in the vegetable garden.

ABOVE When propagating your own plants to create a new border or fill gaps, it is vital that you inject plenty of variety – in terms of shapes and colour – to ensure a varied flow with lots of interesting, eye-catching 'highs' and 'lows'.

Filling gaps

Anyone can rearrange a room and get it right the first time. Try that with a garden. Medium-size plants suddenly become very big, casting those behind in shade, colour combinations that sounded thrilling look positively quotidian, while other plants sit and sulk and refuse to look like their press release. Time to act and rearrange, and with new combinations come new gaps and the need for repeat planting so that the best colours echo throughout the garden, leading the eye to new areas.

Once you have got one key plant, it is usually a simple job to create extra numbers from it. At the simplest level, look for one large, plump specimen, and immediately divide it into several more. One perennial could yield three or four plants immediately if you gently tease it

ABOVE Strawberries are one of the easiest plants to propagate because they virtually do all the work for you, sending out runners. Once they have rooted, sever the link and use the young plants to fill any gaps.

LEFT From a spring sowing you can get a vegetable bed that is packed with produce, keeping you going right through summer.

LEFT The greenhouse is the engine room of the garden, where everything begins. Buy the biggest greenhouse you can because once you start growing your own plants, you will always find scores of new varieties to try.

Replacing mature plants

Some plants fire up so much growth that they gradually become congested in the centre and die out. In the wild they have space to expand, with the new growth occurring at the fringes, but, in a beautifully crafted border where everything has to earn its place, who wants a plant with gappy, poor growth in the middle? Again, dividing a plant to use the fresh, new, vigorous outer growth means that you get new plants for elsewhere in the garden, and can replace the old, poorly performing one. Other plants do not just die out in the centre; they die out altogether after a few years. They have a short shelf-life. Others become so big that they need to be thrown out and replaced by a younger version. Being able to propagate means that you will always have a solution to these problems.

apart or use a knife to slice it up, making sure that each new plant has the two basics needed for survival: a good root system to drink and feed and anchor it in the ground, and good top growth for photosynthesis, a self-powering chain reaction using energy from sunlight.

Dividing is what is called vegetative propagation – and that involves every kind of technique except for seed sowing. You are basically creating new, uniform plants from a grown, established plant, using anything from a division to a severed root, leaf or shoot. Shoots are certainly one the easiest ways of growing new plants and plugging gaps. Just nip off new, young, non-flowering shoots that are growing strongly and plant each shoot in a small container. They will soon root, grow and branch out.

Some shoots do not need to be immediately severed from the parent to create a new plant. When they come in contact with soil, they tend to root where they are, which is why a sucker (spearing out of the ground from part of the parent plant, beneath the soil) can be left to get a good root system before it is then used as a new plant. If the top growth of other plants is bent to the ground and pinned in place, or is left growing when covered in piles of soil, it too will root and can eventually be severed to make a healthy, substantial new plant. All can be used to flesh out a border.

RIGHT A traditional spring-bedding scene with standard roses above rows of tulips. As soon as the latter have faded, they can be dug up and replaced by newly sown summer annuals.

ABOVE Once you have raised your first batch of poppies, collect their seed for next year.

Growing a wider range of crops

If you want a productive kitchen garden, no matter what size, you have got to learn the basics of seed propagation because crops such as beans, carrots, courgettes, cucumbers, leeks, lettuces and tomatoes are all grown from (ideally fresh) packets of seed. All of these annuals grow like a typical flower (see Anatomy of a Plant), producing a good set of feeding roots – which will also stabilize the plant in the ground – and stems or leafy growth. Some flower before they crop (e.g. courgettes and tomatoes), providing us with the tasty, fleshy covering around a batch of seeds, while others (e.g. lettuces) must be eaten before they start to flower. Once a lettuce does this (called 'bolting'), the taste becomes too sharp and bitter.

Sexual reproduction

In general, the best way to get an exact copy of a plant is by vegetative propagation. Some plants do not set viable seed in cool climates (*Stipa gigantea*), many with double flowers

ANATOMY OF A PLANT

Knowing the names of the main structures of a plant is important for an understanding of the techniques described in this book. This illustration shows a typical plant, with the below-ground feeding, anchoring root system and the flowering, photosynthesizing top growth.

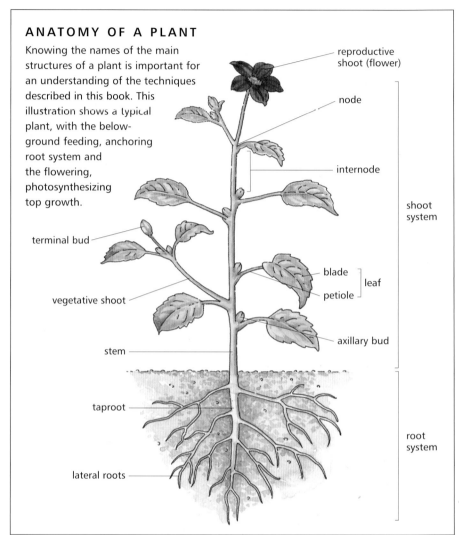

ABOVE The species crocus *Crocus tommasinianus* will self-seed freely to produce prodigious sheets of flowers in spring. It naturalizes easily in grass and thrives in light woodland.

ABOVE A very practical cold frame with high light levels for raising young plants. The large shape allows the plants to be spaced out nicely, giving good air circulation.

ABOVE An impressive display of border wallflowers can be easily raised from seed.

tend to be sterile (primroses), some need a separate male and female plant (most hollies), and the seed of most cultivars will not recreate the parent exactly, although there are always some exceptions (including *Borago officinalis* 'Alba', *Lobelia* 'Queen Victoria' and *Viola* 'Bowles Black'). Because seed carries the genetic characteristics of two parents, there is inbuilt variety. That is good news for the plants and for us.

Genetic diversity increases the likelihood of survival when the environment might change, and it might make a species even more successful in its existing environment. You might well find a seedling in the garden that is a new, absolute beauty. Plant breeders are constantly trying to find newer, better plants with more disease resistance, longevity, scent, weather resistance and ease of growing, allied to an attractive shape and a long season of good colour (with excellent yield, taste and storage in the case of crops). They are trying to engineer plants that sell

well. Most plants grown in gardens are basically wild plants that have been modified by humans. Some are modified by nature when a genetic change causes a mutation, a typical example being a shoot with variegated leaves. If a gardener sees a branch with beautifully variegated leaves, they can take a cutting and, with luck, be able to name the new, best-selling cultivar something like 'Now I'm Rich'. Propagation does not just keep the garden alive, it keeps gardening alive with new possibilities.

In this book

No matter what kind of plant you want to raise, each stage of the propagation process is described in this book, so you will know what to do and when. Of course, there is no point in propagating unless you can raise the new young plants properly, so the book begins with a guide to basic equipment, as well as information to help you understand your garden soil. Then come the six key areas: propagating by seed, cuttings, division, propagating

underground storage organs (bulbs, tubers and corms), layering and grafting. There is a useful summary of the pests and diseases you may encounter at the back of the book, and a glossary of terms will help you understand the specialist techniques.

ABOVE A collection of young plants being raised in a large, light, airy polytunnel.

Getting started

You can propagate plants using just a few pots and bags of compost (soil mix), but the moment you start tackling large numbers of different plants, you will need more equipment. All is readily available, and the only major acquisition is a greenhouse or polytunnel.

Secateurs

Choose the bypass or parrot kind that act like a pair of scissors with two sharp blades slicing past each other giving a good, clean cut. Anvil secateurs instead rely on one blade cutting down on to a softer piece of metal, inevitably crushing and damaging the stem in the process. Price is a good indication of quality, but a good pair will last many years, especially if well maintained. Many manufacturers run a repair-and-sharpen service, or sell spare parts. Avoid using secateurs for any purpose other than taking cuttings and pruning, and never use them to cut wire, even if it means a lengthy walk back to the garden shed for wire cutters. Keep them regularly cleaned, oiled and sharpened.

Knives (garden, budding, grafting, scalpel)

Knives give a good, clean cut when taking cuttings, without any chance of damaging the stem tissue, reducing the chances of successful

ABOVE Biodegradable containers

propagation. All need to be regularly sharpened and cleaned. Cut toward yourself for maximum control.

Containers

The range of containers includes plastic seed trays with clear plastic covers or lids, pots (biodegradable and plastic), root trainers, modules and even lengths of guttering. Seed trays are the best option when you are sowing large numbers of a

particular plant, but pricking out tight, congested clumps can be tricky so try to space out the seedlings when sowing. Do not delay pricking out, because you will end up with a mass of intermingling, knotted roots that grow down and then out horizontally, making separation very difficult. Pots are ideal for small numbers of seed, the best option being plastic because it is durable, light and quick to wash clean. Biodegradable pots, made from compressed peat or wood fibre, are ideal for plants that hate root disturbance. When the roots poke out of the sides and bottom, you simply put the pot and the seedling in a bigger container and fill in with compost (soil mix), although biodegradable pots can badly dry out or, conversely, go mouldy if kept too wet. Clay pots are certainly more attractive but are more expensive and

LEFT Plastic and terracotta containers

ABOVE Plastic modules

ABOVE Root trainers

ABOVE Secateurs

ABOVE Scalpel

ABOVE Soil sieve

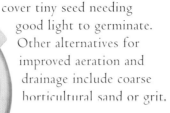

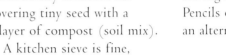

ABOVE Horticultural sand and grit

cover tiny seed needing good light to germinate. Other alternatives for improved aeration and drainage include coarse horticultural sand or grit.

Soil sieve

Absolutely essential for covering tiny seed with a fine layer of compost (soil mix). A kitchen sieve is fine, separating the chaff from the dust.

Rooting powder

Most cuttings readily produce their own roots at the severed bottom end, ideally just below a node, but

LEFT Dibber

you can dip them in rooting powder (also available as a liquid) to encourage good results. Always tap off any excess.

Dibber

A pointed tool for making holes in compost (soil mix) or soil when sowing seed and inserting seedlings. Pencils or crayons can be used as an alternative.

Labels

All too easily overlooked, but inexpensive, stiff white plastic labels are absolutely invaluable (though the pencil writing eventually fades) for recording what has been sown and when. Always buy more than you need because there is nothing worse than planting up several seed trays and suddenly finding you've none left.

dry out quicker, losing moisture through evaporation via the sides. Root trainers (with hinged compartments) encourage deep roots that are not disturbed, and can be used for getting vegetables such as lettuces and beans off to an early start, growing them under cover for planting out the moment the weather is right, as well as for deep-rooted trees and shrubs. Modules (which are not hinged) also enable you to grow seedlings in separate compartments so that when they are potted on there's no root disturbance.

Drainage material

Seed needs to be grown in aerated, free-draining material, and it is worth adding some light perlite (sterile, inert rock granules). Similar vermiculite holds more water but less air. Both can also be used to just

ABOVE Perlite

ABOVE Vermiculite

ABOVE Rooting powder

ABOVE Labels

ABOVE An upturned rose spray, arching a fine shower that will not damage young seedlings.

ABOVE The most useful propagators, such as the one shown here, have a range of temperature settings. More limited types are unheated, with a seed tray and a clear plastic lid.

Watering can

The most important prerequisite is the fine rose spray that can be turned face-up so that the spray arches up and then down in fine drops. Do not ruin a good batch of seedlings by sending a heavy bombardment of great big water drops straight down, which will batter and crush the weak stems and disturb the compost. Alternatively, stand small pots or seed trays in a large pan of water so that it soaks up, or use a special sprayer, holding several litres of water, with an adjustable nozzle that gives a fine misting and a good soaking.

Clear plastic bags

Excellent for slipping seed trays or pots inside to create a warm, humid atmosphere when germinating seed. The moment growth appears, promptly remove.

Propagator

Available in various sizes with varying degrees of sophistication (prices vary accordingly), they provide the warmth and humidity necessary to raise large numbers of plants. The temperature is electronically controlled. DIY kinds can be made using soil-warming cable. Always go for a large size.

Cold frame

The intermediate stage between a protected warm environment and life outdoors, where seedlings are hardened off and toughened up, and hardy seeds can be given a winter chilling. The term is a good literal description – a solid, unheated frame or low wall surrounds the plants, while a hinged, transparent lid can be closed or opened according to the weather.

Cloche

A traditional, portable means of protecting seedlings growing out in the open, and warming the soil. Use it to get crops off to an early

ABOVE It is very easy to create your own, very effective DIY propagator using just a pot and a large, clear plastic covering.

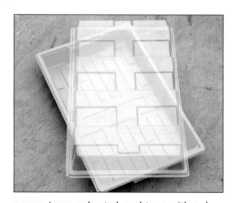

ABOVE Large unheated seed trays with a clear lid are ideal for raising hardy annuals and cuttings that do not need bottom heat.

ABOVE See-through cold frames might not be as strong as those with brick sides, but they let in more light. Stand in a sheltered place.

ABOVE A small cloche can double as a mini cold frame for just a few plants, or be used to cover an early crop until the weather improves.

ABOVE The advantage of a sunny, lean-to greenhouse is that the inside brick wall bounces back heat, ideal for producing grapes and figs.

start. Made from short metal hoops covered with clear plastic or glass. Remove immediately once the weather permits.

Nursery bed

A useful area, space permitting, where young plants can be grown until they are large enough to be planted out in their final position.

Greenhouse

The engine room of the garden, a greenhouse is almost a necessity. You can just about get by without

ABOVE In the kitchen garden, you can use an ornamental bell jar for covering and protecting a young plant in its final position.

one by raising young plants on a sunny windowsill, but there will not be room for many, and it can be a major inconvenience. The best advice is to decide what size greenhouse you need, and then buy one that is even bigger, providing a larger working space. The big choice is between aluminium, brick and wood, and the polytunnel. Aluminium is the easiest to care for with excellent interior light levels. Wood is more attractive, but casts more shade and needs some upkeep unless expensive cedar frames are used. Brick also looks attractive, and solid, but you can lose a lot of light to about waist height. Polytunnels are the most inexpensive option, but they are not that attractive, can be costly to heat (therefore are often used unheated), and might need running repairs to the fabric. In all cases look for internal structures that will provide supports for climbers. Also beware the build-up of pests and diseases, and note the need for good hygiene and summer ventilation, using side and roof vents in the greenhouse with shading, because temperatures inside can

rocket. Heated greenhouses obviously increase your growing options, especially with regard to tender plants, with electric heaters being easier than gas because of the need for ventilation to avoid the build-up of fumes and condensation. Paraffin heaters have several drawbacks (fumes and condensation), and need regular attention, but make a good emergency option. Being able to attach bubble plastic insulation in winter can make a big difference. Finally, stand the greenhouse away from trees and shade.

ABOVE Some containers are available with clear plastic domes that act like a mini-cloche to protect young plants.

Knowing your garden soil

You will never grow good plants unless you can grow them in the kind of soil they need. With new gardens, do check what kind of soil you've got, and if it is completely inappropriate for your crops, start improving it. You can have the best plants in the world, but if they're rooted in poor or the wrong soil, they will be an amazing let-down.

Plants' needs

Most soil was originally rock that has gradually been weathered and ground down over the centuries, and the kind of soil you have in your garden depends on which kind of rock it came from. The soil provides your plants with nutrients, and while it is possible to grow plants without any soil at all (using a technique called hydroponics), you will then have to make sure they're fed. Food is vital. Plant roots also need oxygen, found in the gaps between the soil particles, and water. Surprisingly,

ABOVE Before planting a border, check that you've got the right soil for your plants. Most summer annuals and perennials need free-draining ground, enriched with organic matter.

most root growth takes place in the top 10–15cm (4–6in) of soil, and even the roots of huge, mature trees rarely go deep, with well over 90 per cent well within the top 100cm (40in). They provide stability by

fanning out, also absorbing every bit of rain that soaks through the ground beneath the outer edge of the canopy. That is why few plants perform well beneath a tree because its massive network of near-horizontal roots are feeding on the nutrients in the top layer, quickly absorbing the moisture. It is also worth stressing that soil, as

SOIL PROFILE

The soil beneath trees will not suit all kinds of plants. This is because the extensive spreading root system is mainly found in the top layers, and it quickly absorbs the moisture and nutrients. The added shade from the canopy means that woodland-type plants – e.g. ivy (*Hedera hibernica*) – have the best chance of thriving.

topsoil

subsoil

parent material

ABOVE To get a large crop of tomatoes, start regularly feeding the plant with potassium once the first batch of fruit has set.

ABOVE To create extra fruit-bearing branches on a chilli plant, give it an early feed of nitrogen.

Nutrient deficiencies

- Nitrogen – yellow foliage, especially lower down, accompanied by feeble growth with reduced branching.
- Phosphorus – poor growth with dull yellow leaves.
- Potassium – discoloured leaves that acquire purple, blue or yellow tints with brown blotching, and generally poor performance.
- Calcium – cupped leaf tips while the young leaves turn black.
- Magnesium – mottled yellowing on older leaves between the veins. Typically occurs when plants needing acid (or ericaceous) soil are grown on alkaline soil.
- Sulphur – stiff, erect foliage and new yellow leaves. Also often occurs when acid-loving plants are grown in alkaline soil.

To bolster nitrogen levels, use sulphate of ammonia or pelleted poultry manure, adding sulphate of potash to improve potassium levels, and superphosphate in the case of poor phosphorus levels. Magnesium and sulphur problems are often remedied by growing acid-loving plants in the correct soil, while extra magnesium is provided in the form of Epsom salts or magnesium sulphate.

mentioned, stabilizes plants in the ground, and provides a buffer against adverse temperature changes. When putting new plants in the ground, always firm them in well.

Nutrients

The six main soil nutrients essential for good plant growth are:

- Nitrogen
- Phosphorus
- Potassium
- Calcium
- Magnesium
- Sulphur

with boron, chlorine, copper, iron, manganese, molybdenum, nickel and zinc helping, while some plants also benefit from cobalt, silicon and sodium. The first three on the list are the most important. Nitrogen (called N on packets of fertilizer) promotes soft, leafy growth and determines the amount of growth a plant can make. Nitrogen levels are invariably low at the start of spring because so much has been sluiced out of the ground by winter rain, but bacterial activity

ensures that levels rise by the end of summer. It is very tempting to force feed leafy vegetables with plenty of nitrogen to generate even more growth, but too much soft growth can make them vulnerable to disease. They also need phosphorus (or P), which is vital in generating root growth. The third of the major nutrients is potassium (K), which boosts disease-resistant growth and, crucially, flower and fruit

development, which is why so much is bought each year for crops such as tomato plants to generate bigger fruit. Gardens rarely face any shortage of phosphorus (the possible exception being heavy clay after heavy rain) or potassium (possible exceptions being confined to light, sandy, or chalky soil following heavy winter deluges), but it is worth noting the possible symptoms should such cases arise.

LEFT Pale green or yellowish chlorotic leaves can be caused by mineral deficiencies, especially with excess lime, or poor light.

BELOW Plants are very quick to tell us when they are stressed. This badly neglected plant needs repotting and a good drink.

Fertilizer

Most gardens need only an all-purpose feed (that will last a few weeks) lightly forked into the soil a few weeks before planting. This boosts the plants in all the key areas (i.e. root, stem, leaf and flower growth). The strength of the feed is denoted by an NPK reading. So, 5:8:10 indicates 5 percent nitrogen, 8 of phosphorus and 10 of potassium, making it ideal for fruiting plants, such as tomatoes. 'Growmore' is an inorganic compound fertilizer, its organic counterpart being fish, blood and bone. For a quick nutrient boost, use a liquid form that is watered directly into the soil, where it can be taken up by the plants' roots.

Manure and compost

Also a valuable source of N, P and K, manure must be at least three months old before being used. However, you will not know how much N, P and K are contained, and this depends on the animals involved and their bedding.

RIGHT Worms are an essential part of the garden, helping to churn up a compost heap, while getting in extra oxygen.

IMPROVING THE SOIL

1 When adding organic matter to improve garden soil, use a fork to ensure that the two are thoroughly mixed.

2 When adding non-organic fertilizer to the soil, carefully follow the manufacturer's instructions and apply the correct amount.

3 When putting in new plants, take the opportunity to improve the soil by adding compost to the planting hole.

4 Apply a mulch twice a year, in spring and autumn, to help keep down weeds, keep the soil moist and protect plants' roots.

Well-rotted compost has poor nutrient levels but it is excellent in other ways. It is an incredibly good way of improving the soil structure, making it dark, crumbly and workable, especially where you have an extreme soil (for example, heavy clay or sand or chalk), thereby benefiting soil life, and of improving the water-holding capacity. Aim to add one full bucket to every $1m^2$ (10sq ft).

Compost is also extremely valuable as a mulch. Pile it over the soil about 6cm (2½ in) deep in spring to block out any weeds and lock moisture into the ground, stopping it from quickly evaporating (which is why it is best applied after a night of heavy rain). In time it will break down, thereby also improving the soil. An autumn-winter mulch is invaluable because it will help insulate the plants' roots, protecting them from extreme temperatures.

Earthworms are also attracted to compost, and their presence is vital: they open up the soil, improving oxygen levels and drainage, and pulling organic matter on the surface underground.

DIY compost in 6 months

For your compost bin you have two basic choices, either bought (usually made from plastic, but sometimes wood) or home-made. If you only need small amounts, just one bin is fine, otherwise use three larger bins, each holding 750–1,000 litres (26½–35cu ft). One is used for filling, one will have been already filled and is 'cooking', while the third is used for spreading. Site the bins in a sunny position on forked up ground, giving good drainage and ensuring the presence of earthworms. If making your own bin, use wooden planks, at least 2.5cm (1in) thick.

All are nailed permanently in place to stout posts, except for the front ones, so that you can remove these and turn the compost over with a fork to aerate it. Also add a removable wooden 'lid' to keep the heap dry.

Fill your finished compost bin with shredded woody material (paper, cardboard and dead leaves, etc.) well mixed with about 35–45 per cent of kitchen waste, grass clippings, annual weeds, etc. When dry, sprinkle with water, and do not let any one ingredient dominate. Avoid adding materials such as cooked food which attracts rats, perennial weeds and diseased plants.

ABOVE A compost heap divided by walls into good-sized sections. The sturdy walls can be made from horizontal railway sleepers held in place by stout posts. It is important that there is plenty of room for the gardener to step into each pile and turn it over, getting in plenty of oxygen. A potential problem with such large compartments is keeping the material dry during wet weather.

LEFT A purpose-made compost bin. The door at the base allows you to remove the compost.

TURNING A COMPOST HEAP

1 Start from the front or back of the heap and work toward the other end. You want to make sure that every part is turned.

2 Take a large forkful and lift it up, exposing the area beneath. Turning a heap is more than just rearranging the surface.

3 Toss each clump up and down, getting in plenty of air, preventing the pile from becoming a solid, stagnant heap.

Soil types

Different soils have different characteristics, and it is important to know what you are working with. It is very easy to determine what kind of soil you have simply by holding it in your hand. The two extremes are:

• Clay – the tiny particles stick together enabling you to roll it into a sticky ball that keeps its shape. The good news is that it is potentially fertile, but drainage will be poor, and it takes a long time to warm up in spring. When dry, clay soil is inclined to form cracks on the surface; when it rains it swells and stays sopping wet. Heavy clay soil is also incredibly hard work when it comes to digging and weeding, being more like concrete in summer. It is, however, easily improved by adding composted organic matter, including composted bark and mushroom compost, and horticultural (or 'sharp') grit. Note that mushroom compost is alkaline and should not be used with acid-loving plants.

• Sandy – in complete contrast, it is gritty, light and free-draining with poor nutrient levels, and needs improving by adding lots of well-rotted compost on a regular basis to

The 'no-dig' philosophy

Organic gardeners dislike digging up beds, taking the 'no-dig' approach. The advantages are that weed seed is not brought to the surface, the soil structure stays intact and nutrient levels remain consistent. The 'no-dig' approach also relies heavily on earthworm activity (which is disrupted by deep digging) and organic mulches, which means that all the action is taking place near the surface. So, there's no danger of the topsoil (with the good water-retention of its organic matter) and the much poorer subsoil getting mixed up when digging. To be really effective, 'no-dig' should be reserved for areas with weed-free, light, free-draining soil. In effect, everyone practises this system in the flower garden. Once beds have been dug up with organic material added, they are not tampered with except when holes are 'trowelled out' for new plants. Some gardeners like to dig larger holes than necessary, using the opportunity to add extra quantities of well-rotted organic compost, but even then this is a relatively small amount of digging compared to the vegetable garden that is traditionally dug up and churned over, sometimes several times, in winter. A good compromise is to 'no-dig' the vegetable patch every other year or so.

improve its moisture- and nutrient-holding capacity. This is particularly important if you are growing hungry plants such as roses.

Other soil types include:

• Chalk – it is obvious by the presence of chalky lumps, making the soil very free draining. Again, it can be improved by adding compost.

• Loam – the ideal soil, but all too rarely found, it clings loosely together and consists of clay, sand and silt.

Alkalinity, acidity and pH

It is important to know the pH of your soil, because this determines what kind of plants you can grow. If your neighbours grow azaleas, rhododendrons and camellias then the soil is acid, but use a simple pH testing kit to get an accurate reading.

Testing kits come in two kinds: the meter (see the pH test, right) and the colour chart. The latter involves taking a soil sample and mixing it in a test tube with distilled water. Give the tube a firm shake and

RECOGNIZING CLAY, SANDY AND LOAMY SOILS

ABOVE Clay is immediately recognizable, readily forming solid lumps of soil. Press your thumb in and it will leave a clear imprint.

ABOVE Sandy soil is the complete opposite, being open, crumbly and friable. It is easy to work but lacks nutrients.

ABOVE Loam, with a mix of nutritious clay and sand which provides good drainage is what everyone wants but few gardens offer.

LEFT To grow rhododendrons like this, you need a garden with acid soil.

BELOW If you cannot provide acid soil, you must grow the rhododendron in a large container filled with special ericaceous (acid) compost (soil mix).

let the mixture settle. Finally, check the colour of the water against the provided colour chart which gives readings which run from 0 to 14. Note that the pH readings may well vary in different parts of the garden.

Neutral soil has a pH of 7, and most plants will thrive in it; acid readings are below that; and alkaline above it. The higher the reading, the greater the calcium levels. If you have alkaline soil, the best way of growing acid-loving plants is in containers or raised beds filled with ericaceous soil. You can reduce the acidity by adding lime.

pH TESTING

1 The best way to test the pH levels is to take samples from different sites in the garden, digging holes and wetting them.

2 Then trowel the wet soil, getting out any stones, from the first hole and slide it into a container, ready for checking.

ABOVE If the soil has too much lime, plants quickly signal the problem because their leaves turn sickly yellow.

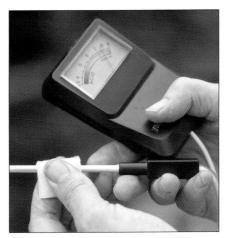

3 Push the switch on the meter to give a pH reading, because many also provide fertility readings.

4 Gently insert the probe into the soil – carefully in case there are still stones in there which might damage it – to find the soil's pH.

Seed Propagation

You cannot propagate plants without trying your hand at sowing seed. It is absolutely essential for growing crops in the vegetable garden – everything from tomatoes and sweet corn to chillies and climbing courgettes – trying out tasty new varieties which you will never get in the supermarkets, and for filling gaps in beds and borders with quick-growing, fun annuals. You can even devote whole beds to annuals, creating interlocking blocks and drifts of bright colours and strong scents, getting a high-voltage, inexpensive display. Growing annuals from seed is perfect for gardeners who get itchy fingers in spring and cannot wait to get going before the temperatures outside have warmed up. Growing annuals also gives you a chance to keep experimenting, trying out different colour combinations and scouring the seed catalogues for the latest introductions.

The following pages tackle every aspect of growing plants from seed, starting with sexual reproduction, the inventive ways in which flowers are pollinated (often tricking insects into lending a hand), how seed spreads to germinate away from the parent, where it has a better chance of surviving without competition for light and nutrients, and the actual act of germination. There is also information about how you can collect seed, and the most effective ways of sowing seed and raising new plants.

LEFT A lively mixture of crops in a potager, all grown from seed, featuring a wide range of shapes and colours.

Sexual reproduction

Plants have evolved extraordinary ways of mating, which basically means transferring pollen from the male to the female parts. This is usually done by insects and/or the wind. But where the wind, and therefore a huge degree of luck, is involved, the plants have to produce even greater amounts of pollen in order to give much better odds of perpetuating themselves.

How do plants reproduce?

Plants can reproduce asexually and vegetatively when they send out runners that root in the ground, or send up suckers around the main plant, for example, producing offspring that is an exact genetic reproduction of the parent. When they reproduce sexually, genetic material from the male and female unites in a seed. The flowers of most plants are bisexual or hermaphrodite. Sometimes a separate, compatible male and female plant are needed (called dioecious), for cross-pollination, and sometimes plants are monoecious, meaning that each individual carries both male and female flowers.

PARTS OF A FLOWER

This close-up of a fuchsia flower clearly shows the male and female reproductive organs. The female reproductive pistil consists of the ovary at the base of the style and the stigma. The male reproductive parts, collectively called the stamen, consist of a pollen-producing anther, usually on a filament.

Some plants are bisexual with the male stamens surrounding the female pistils. When the ovule has been fertilized it develops into seed, which contains enough food to fuel the initial stages of growth.

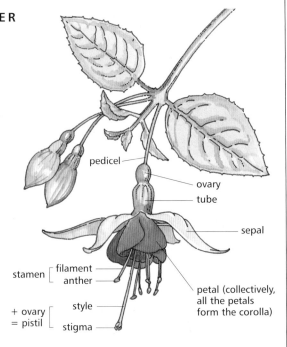

pedicel
ovary
tube
sepal
stamen [filament / anther
style
+ ovary = pistil [stigma
petal (collectively, all the petals form the corolla)

Reproductive structures

The key reproductive parts of angiosperms are kept in the flowers. (Angiosperms are flowering plants whose seed is enclosed in an ovary, unlike the non-flowering gymnosperms, such as conifers, which have naked seeds.) Most flowers, despite their different looks and scents, have the same basic structure, with petals and sepals, whose role is to enclose and protect the inner floral parts. Seed-producing female parts comprise ovaries, and a style that connects the ovary and stigma. The stigma receives the pollen and is usually sticky in order that it safely adheres. The ovary, style and stigma form the pistil. Male parts comprise stamens and pollen-bearing anthers. Hermaphrodite flowers include both male and female parts.

Offspring

The seed has genetic characteristics of both parents, but will not produce offspring that are exact reproductions of the parents. There will be differences, and that is what seed companies continuously investigate in the search for the next big-selling plant. When they can provide seed producing known, uniform plants (particularly important with flowers and

ABOVE We might think it is just a tasty fruit, but an apple is actually a very clever, reliable life-support system. Its prime aim is to help create the next generation of apple trees. The seed will be distributed by animals picking the fruit to eat the flesh.

ABOVE Sweet corn is grown in close groups because it is wind pollinated, with the pollen being blown from the anthers to the stigma.

ABOVE In order to get pollinated by insects, and guarantee the survival of the species, flowers need to provide an eye-catching, colourful and/or scented display. This makes the flower bed a very competitive place, with the different plants vying for attention.

vegetables), it is sold as F1, or the first generation of a cross between known parents. F1 hybrids give good results with vigorous growth, and, in the case of vegetables, large crops, but they are only available for a small percentage of plants, and then mostly annuals. They are tricky to create and are consequently more expensive than ordinary seed.

ABOVE Growing colourful, scented plants is an excellent way of attracting insects, and a house wall covered with a vigorous climbing ivy will erupt in yellowish-green bisexual autumn flowers. They are followed by small, rounded fruits, loved by the wildlife.

ABOVE The tiny pink, purple or white summer flowers of thyme are a major insect magnet, attracting scores of pollinators.

Pollination

This simply means that pollen has been moved from the male anther to the female stigma, and once that happens everything changes. The petals are not needed to attract pollinators, and they fade and fall, revealing the slightly swelling ovary beneath. In the case of an apple tree this becomes the fruit, a juicy, tasty, fleshy, protective case with the seeds within. The seeds themselves are protected from extreme temperature changes and damage by creatures and infection by their own hard outer layer. Most seeds also contain food stores to keep the embryo alive in the soil, and to help it through the seedling stage until it becomes self-sufficient with roots and shoots.

Self- and cross-pollination

Sometimes a single plant actually produces flowers that are either exclusively male or female, sweet corn being the most obvious example. That is why corn is grown in blocks, with the plants in close proximity, about 45cm (18in) apart in the case of taller varieties; the wind blows the pollen from the anthers of the male flowers growing

ABOVE The wide-open flower of a dahlia gives easy access to the sexual organs right in the centre. The petals are called the ray floret and the yellow centre is the disc floret.

at the top of the plant down on to the female stigma growing below, which might be on the same plant or another one. Grow individual plants around the garden, well away from each other, and the chances of getting a crop are severely reduced. Self-pollination, though, is not always in the best interests of some plants, reducing genetic variation, and they have special mechanisms to prevent this happening. The most obvious and most effective involves the male and female parts ripening at different times, a kind of self-imposed segregation. Where self-pollination is important, there is simultaneous ripening.

Animal pollination

The most obvious means of pollen transfer involves the wind (both unpredictable and erratic) and birds, bats and insects (including butterflies, sawflies, wasps, bees,

ABOVE Plants are immobile and cannot go out to find sexual partners, and must attract pollinating insects by colour and scent.

ABOVE The hoverfly feeds on nectar and pollen, and avoids predators by resembling wasps and bees when it is actually just a fly.

ABOVE In midsummer the butterfly bush (*Buddleja davidii*) is covered by long panicles, consisting of scores of tiny scented flowers, attracting pollinating bees and butterflies.

ABOVE The central disc of a sunflower produces copious seed, a food source for birds.

ants, honey and bumble bees), all being attracted by brightly coloured petals, the production of sticky, sugar-rich nectar and nutritious pollen. But while some plants reward their pollinators, others do not. Some orchids trick them. Dancing lady orchids (*Oncidium*) produce

Extra flowers, extra seed

If you want a plant to put out lots of flowers so that you get plentiful seed, grow it in a container, keep it slightly pot bound, put it under stress and it will immediately respond by developing lots of flowers, and seed, trying to propagate. If you want an abundance of attractive flowers from a garden plant, keep taking off the fading ones to thwart the plant's ambition to procreate. It will respond the only way it knows, by developing more flowers (and more seed). If you let the seed develop, the plant will then channel its energy into that. It will not have any need to keep flowering as prolifically.

flowers that resemble an army of bees, and when the real bees see them they charge and attack, so coming into contact with and dispensing the pollen. Other orchids lure pollinators by producing flowers that resemble sexy female moths ready to mate, and even emit a similar scent. More ingeniously, some Mediterranean flowers resemble the rotting flesh of, say, a donkey, with a smell to match, attracting pollinating flies. Some flowers, which only open for the briefest 48-hour spell, put on an incredible show to guarantee they get pollinated quickly, with the Sumatran *Amorphophallus titanum* growing 90cm–1.5m (3–5ft) high with a stink that is just indescribable. But what if there are not any creatures about to carry out the pollination? Fruit trees, for example, produce blossom in spring, but if the weather is too cold for the insects you may have to do it by hand, where possible, on small

trained shapes (for example, espaliers against a wall), using a small paint brush to transfer the pollen to the stigma, to guarantee a good crop. If there is a bad late spring frost, then the blossom will get zapped and you will get a very poor or non-existent crop.

ABOVE Pollinating by hand using a clean brush to transfer the pollen to the stigma, which is often sticky, to make it adhere.

Dispersal mechanisms

The ultimate aim of all plants is to reproduce and expand their territory. The problem is that they are immobile – well, to a point. They might not have legs, but they can certainly travel. Strawberries send out extending shoots called runners that root and produce new plants, while blackberries produce a great colonizing tangle of growth. When it comes to spreading seed to germinate away from the parent, avoiding competition for food and light, plants have found all kinds of ingenious techniques.

Independent spreaders

The Mediterranean sea cucumber (*Ecballium elaterium*) and broom (*Cytisus*) are two of the most inventive seed spreaders. The cucumber has a built-in pressure chamber. It gradually fills with juice as it ripens, until it reaches the critical point when it gets flung from its stalk and whizzes through the air for about 5.4m (18ft). Even better, it trails a mix of slime and seed through a hole, scattering it across the ground. Without help from any external agency, it manages

ABOVE Sea cucumber (*Ecballium elaterium*) likes poor, dry, free-draining ground where it will produce fruits that fling out its seed.

to create expanding colonies of itself. Broom is slightly different and relies on the sun's heat to disperse its seed in different directions. The sides of the pods facing the sun heat up more rapidly than the shady sides, and the internal tension makes the pod burst open and propel its seed away. Legumes also have pods that split on drying with a satisfying snap.

Wind aid

Other plants are dependent on the wind, with poppies producing drying seed heads or capsules with small holes at the top. Prise one head open and you will see that it is packed with masses of seed. As the wind blows the stems, so the heads get tossed and shaken, and the tiny seed goes flying. If you want to scatter the seed in another part of the garden, simply pick the ripe heads and shake them like a salt sprinkler where you want extra colonies. If you want to make sure that at least some will definitely germinate, collect and save it for sowing and raising in pots. Such seed is typically minute

ABOVE The seed heads of a clematis are blown away by the wind, creating distant new plants which will not compete with the parent.

ABOVE Dandelions produce seeds with long, feathery tufts attached to each one. The seed is then dispersed by the wind.

ABOVE The seed head of a broom relies on the sun's heat to create internal tension, which eventually makes it burst open.

ABOVE Most seed heads of a maple spin on the wind and land away from the parent, avoiding the dark shade at the base.

ABOVE When the seed pods of a pond iris break open, those tumbling into the water will float away to germinate on a muddy bank.

ABOVE The sticky goosegrass (*Galium aparine*) is designed to latch on to passing creatures, helping the seed to spread far and wide.

ABOVE Agapanthus seed heads, just about to scatter seed on the wind. In cold climates the seed is best saved and sown indoors.

(so that it is easily whipped away on a breeze) and produced on an amazing scale, increasing the odds that some will land where it can safely germinate.

The spinners

Sycamores (*Acer pseudoplatanus*) and maples (*Acer*) are slightly more inventive and produce one-winged seeds that twist and spin through the air like crazily out of control helicopters. Look inside the sycamore's nut with a hand-held lens and you will see an embryo (which is inside every seed) with two pale green seed leaves (cotyledons) tightly rolled up, waiting to develop. The Asiatic *Anisoptera* has a twin-winged seed, but because the wings are not symmetrical they lurch and spin, and whip the seed away from the parent to a place where it can start to germinate. What we regard as the wonderful silvery seed heads of a clematis are also very efficient kinds of seed dispersal. Plants such as *Clematis tangutica* are partly grown for their spidery seed heads that always get a double approving look

when they catch the sun, but their purpose is not to amaze. The fluffy contraptions get caught by the slightest puff of wind, getting wafted away for incredible distances. The crack willow (*Salix fragilis*) propagates itself by cuttings, sending snapped off twigs flying through the air which root in muddy ground.

Fertile willow

Salix can be so quick to propagate that even tree stakes have been known to take root in wet ground, as can sliced-up horizontal sections of a trunk, that have been arranged on bare soil to make a path.

ABOVE *Clematis tangutica* produces yellow summer flowers followed by silvery seed heads that are easily dispersed by the wind.

ABOVE The crack willow (*Salix fragilis*) is very efficient at reproducing itself, with snapped twigs taking root in damp ground.

Animal digestion

When you plant berrying shrubs for the birds to eat in autumn and winter, you're not only helping them; you're also helping the plants to propagate themselves. Jays carry off acorns and drop them en route to wherever. Birds also eat the ripe fruit and berries, and the seeds pass undamaged straight through the gut and out, being deposited in the droppings well away from the parents where, with luck, they will have more space and light to grow and thrive without competition.

Unripened fruit is too bitter to eat, and is only edible when the seed itself has fully developed. When this happens the fruit signals that it is edible, becomes highly coloured (often turning red as with apples and most tomatoes), the texture softens as starch is converted to sugars, and it often gives off a sweet scent. The moment animals see what is happening, they pounce. They learn to read the signals.

Animal hitchhiking

If you've ever wondered why pets come in at night covered in tiny sticky little balls, the seed heads

ABOVE The brightly coloured, highly visible autumn berries of a hawthorn (*Crataegus*) are a boon to birds; they eat the crop and distribute the seeds far and wide in their faeces.

belong to goosegrass (*Galium aparine*). The heads stick to passing creatures and get carried away to fall off and eventually germinate, a very effective means of distributing the species over great distances and in different directions.

Other means of getting a lift over long distances include seed heads with hooks and spines that latch on to passing traffic. But what happens

when a creature that helps transport the seed of a particular plant is wiped out and becomes extinct? The plant might be wiped out too. It is also worth stressing that being transported by an animal can be a

For animals only

The large tropical Malaysian tree *Durio zibethinus* combines prickly, warty thorns and a splendid green capsule (a 'durion') like a large melon on the trunk, and the smell is quite repellent (to us, but not to animals). The flesh is a delicacy and available in Asian markets, but it is banned by airlines. You would not want to be locked up in a metal tube with it!

Nor with the wooden fruit of the *Couroupita guianensis*. Because it grows straight out of the trunk and can be 20cm (8in) wide, it is often called the cannonball tree. The smell of the pulp, for humans, is vile, but wild pigs cannot get enough of it. The seeds have a hairy covering that protects them from the pigs' digestive juices, and they can even germinate in their faeces.

ABOVE The crop of berries with the seed inside is 'flagged' to hungry birds, with the red contrasted against a pale background.

ABOVE If you want to collect seed to sow your own plants, you will have to be quick off the mark to get it before the birds.

risky strategy, which is partly why a surprisingly large number of plants and fruits are toxic, which ensures that they will not get eaten. They have an amazingly efficient deterrent. Yew leaves and twigs are certainly bad news for horses and cows – but it is the seed which is the most poisonous element, not the red fleshy part around it, in extreme cases leading to respiratory failure. Even chippings and fallen leaves lying in a field are dangerously toxic.

Tree seed

Some seed pods are designed to float, and the buoyant, waterproof coconut (*Cocos nucifera*) is the ultimate little boat complete with a life support system capable of drifting for hundreds of miles. The seed inside has an instant supply of liquid and food. When it reaches land it germinates on the shore. But it is not always that easy for trees to spread quickly by seed.

Some, like elms (*Ulmus*), seldom produce viable seed, and oaks (*Quercus*) often produce huge crops only after a long interval. Some seeds, such as ash (*Fraxinus*) and lime (*Tilia*), only germinate after a two- or three-year period, and others might need light – for example, oak – or shade – for example, beech (*Fagus*). In fact few trees can germinate in the shade of the same species.

But when it comes to colonizing new ground, suckering is just about the most efficient technique. Some trees send up suckers, and they in turn sucker, spawning more suckers, and so on, and gradually a huge area is colonized until what looks like a small wood is actually just one ever-spreading, incredibly prolific,

ABOVE The native British yew makes good topiary but it also has high levels of taxin, a complex mixture of toxic alkaloids.

ancient tree. Just one expanding, multiplying, colonizing aspen (*Populus tremuloides*) in Utah, USA, is thought to cover 106 acres (43 hectares). Other trees create the same effect in response to cutting. A giant ash in Essex, England, over 800 years old in the 1970s, responded to centuries of cutting by producing a great ring of new growth, totalling about 20 stems, around the hollow centre.

ABOVE The burdock produces seed heads with tiny specialized hooks that catch in the fur of passing mammals for easy distribution.

ABOVE Aquilegias have highly distinctive, upright seed heads which eventually ripen and split to scatter the shiny black seed.

ABOVE The North American *Populus tremuloides* spreads and regenerates itself thanks to new suckering growth.

Germination

What converts a seed – apparently completely inert, dehydrated tissue, sometimes so small you can scatter scores of them on a finger nail – into a powerful living plant, capable of drawing up over 500 litres (110 gallons) of water a day, in the case of a mature oak? One process: germination.

The four key factors

Seeds, each containing the embryo of a plant, will not germinate until the surface conditions are right, and they generally need four environmental factors to come to life: water and oxygen, temperature and then light.

Water and oxygen

Penetrating the seed coat, water causes swelling while dissolving nutrients that kick-start the growth process. Because seeds are hygroscopic (expanding when wet, almost doubling in size, and conversely contracting when dry), the availability or absence of water is crucial. It is vital that the soil is kept moist after sowing, but if seed

Timing

Germination times of different plants vary considerably, with the quickest seeds to respond usually coming from the most arid areas of the world where, after a sudden bout of heavy rain, it is in the plant's interests to get its roots quickly into the wet soil and start growing before it completely evaporates.

is continuously locked in sopping wet soil then germination will be tricky because there will be severely reduced oxygen levels. Seed needs to breathe. And good oxygen levels are the second factor, helping the seed to release food and energy for the embryo, which is partly why seeds are sown in a light, open, airy compost (soil mix).

Temperature

The third factor is temperature, but this does not mean that if you zap the seeds of various plants with a high temperature they will all germinate. They won't. Different plants have

ABOVE A propagation case with a sliding cover over a ventilation hole provides a safe environment for growing seedlings.

different, often fairly wide maximum and minimum temperature ranges within which germination takes place, with an ideal band in the middle. The temperature at which germination takes place usually

ABOVE What looks like a scattering of insignificant blobs is a mass of seed, each one capable of producing a vigorous plant.

ABOVE Plants are far more adaptable than we imagine, and self-sown seedlings can emerge in even the tiniest nooks and crannies.

ABOVE A powerhouse of a mature tree growing in the best position, well away from other trees competing for light and water.

equates to the spring temperatures found in a plant's native habitat. Consequently, plants from colder temperate regions need lower temperatures to start germinating than plants from the tropics. If you cannot provide artificial heat for temperate seed to match late spring-time temperatures outdoors, just keep seed trays on a sunny windowsill in mid-spring, where the temperature should be about 15°C (60°F), and you will still get early growth. If you provide temperatures that exceed a seed's ideal range, you will probably get thin, feeble, tall growth or possibly no growth at all.

ABOVE Phlox seeds quickly germinate within a period of 7–10 days, with perennials flowering in their second year.

ABOVE Leave the heads on 'drumstick' alliums when the flowers fade, either for gathering seed or because of their attractive shape.

Light

The fourth factor is light, in combination with rising temperatures. As a good guide, sow seed to the depth of one seed placed on top of it. So, small seed will be near the surface (and some seed is so fine that you can just cover it with perlite or vermiculite), while large seed goes deeper in the ground. Plant fine seed so deeply that light levels are excluded and it will not germinate. (As ever, there are some exceptions; *Allium* and phlox, for example, germinate only when there is no light.) Provided you are sensible and follow the directions on the packet of seed, light levels will not be a problem. Never leave seed on the surface in the garden because it will promptly get taken by birds and mice.

Built-in repair kit

The first visible signs of seed growth follow imbibition, a process that prompts the swelling of the seed's tissues. This causes the seed coat to split, letting in both water and gases. As the cells hydrate, nutrients are transferred to the embryo, but some of the early activity in a seed is required to repair damage caused by drying.

ABOVE Seeds need light, water, oxygen and warmth to germinate, with room to grow separate, not entangled, root systems.

RIGHT Once the seeds have germinated, they must be separated into individual compartments giving them extra space.

ABOVE Sandpapering seeds with a tough outer covering helps water get in to kick-start the germination process.

ABOVE Alternatively the toughest seed coverings can be nicked with the point of a clean, sharp knife to let in moisture.

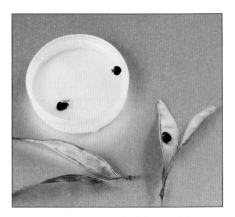

ABOVE Many seeds can be left overnight in a bowl of warm water, prompting the seed to swell and split.

Dormancy

When seeds have been shed, they lie dormant in the soil waiting for the surface conditions to favour successful growth. That is their whole *raison d'être*. But sometimes their needs do not coincide with our needs, or with conditions in the garden. For example, some alpine seed needs a cold period before it will germinate, and other seeds are programmed to develop at staggered times to give better germination rates and perpetuate the species. There are several techniques for helping seeds break dormancy, depending on the nature of the problem.

ABOVE Laburnum species can be grown from seed. It needs to be sown in a container in autumn, which is then placed in a cold frame.

Scarification

The problem with tough, impermeable seed coats, for example the seed of broom (*Cytisus*), *Gleditsia* and *Laburnum*, is that is that they cannot be penetrated immediately by water. The tough coating inhibits quick and even germination. In the wild that is not a problem – there is no immediate need for speedy germination, and the coat gradually decays over a long period – but in the garden it is. Hence the need for scarification, a technical term for cracking through this suit of armour and letting moisture seep in. You can file seeds with the toughest coats, or nick them with a knife, while others can be rubbed between sheets of sandpaper or, as in the case of sweet peas (*Lathyrus odoratus*), you can soak them overnight in warm water or between wet sheets of kitchen paper. When the case swells, softens and splits you will see a flash of white beneath. Immediately sow before the seeds dry out.

Stratification

Other seeds need a period of winter chilling, called stratification (from the practice of putting the seed in strata of sand, to stop them drying out, in the garden), and this particularly applies to alpines, and hardy trees and shrubs. Put the seeds in a plastic bag with some damp sand and refrigerate them in mid-winter, the length of time (ranging from 4–20 weeks, but usually from 6–8) depending on the size of the seed and its natural habitat. When you can see about one-third of the seeds have developed tiny roots they can

Other forms of dormancy

Some seeds (for example, eucalyptus) only germinate after they have been exposed to sudden searing temperatures as fires flash through the cluttered bushy undergrowth in parts of Australia, for example. The fires break open the tough seed cases, while chemicals in the smoke also help some seeds to germinate. The fires destroy most of the competitive growth, giving the new seedlings a good start in the open, with excellent light levels. Other seeds stay in a period of dormancy until they have passed though an animal's gut where the chemical inhibitor, lining the outer coat of the seed case, gets removed. Other seed – for example, hellebore – has an immature embryo and needs a long warm spell before it develops and germination can occur.

Roots

Plants produce a variety of different roots. Their primary aim is to anchor the plant and allow it to feed and drink, the moisture being pumped up and around the top growth. The first root is the radicle, and it sometimes tunnels deeper and deeper as a taproot, while other plants are distinguished by their multi-branching system of fibrous roots. Some plants (the epiphytes) live attached to other plants and have aerial roots that feed off trapped leaf debris in the absence of soil, and absorb both humidity in the air and falling rain, while others (mistletoe) actually root in tree branches and parasitically feed off the host plant. Adventitious roots appear in unexpected places, for example bursting out of a main stem.

ABOVE Eucalyptus are primed to grow very quickly, and take advantage of sudden gaps in the Australian bush caused by fires.

ABOVE Look closely at any ivy growing up a tree or wall and you will see scores of tiny hair-like roots growing out from the stems.

be removed from the bag for sowing. Alternatively, you can just scatter the seed on top of the compost (soil mix) in a pot, and then cover it with sand. Leave it out in an exposed place where it can get frosted, but make sure that the pot will not go flying in a gale. The worse the conditions, the better. That's what it would face in the wild.

Early growth

When growing different kinds of seed, the first thing you notice is that the seedlings emerge in different ways. Courgette seedlings push up, out of the compost (soil mix), with the opened seed case clamped over the leaves. As the leaves open, so they fling it off. Do not be tempted to prise off the case because

you might well damage the tender young leaves. The roots are attached to the base of the seedling. This is called epigeal germination, unlike hypogeal germination where the seed case and the seed leaves (or cotyledons) are left under the soil, with the seedling growing vertically up out of it, and roots growing down out of the bottom.

LEFT Look on the soil around a hellebore and you will find seedlings that can be potted up. Only keep those with the best flowers.

BELOW Courgette seeds shoot up, so do not sow until several weeks before planting out or you will have nowhere to put them.

Collecting and saving seed

If you've got a particularly good species plant in the garden that can be propagated by sowing seed, collect some when it has ripened. Many plants do the job for you, scattering seed, and all you've got to do is carefully lift the seedlings and plant them where required. But to guarantee that happens, try the following techniques.

Gathering seed

The best time to collect seed from healthy, vigorous plants is usually when the seed is ripe. Stick the seed head in a paper bag and give it a good shake until all the seed has fallen out. Collect from species plants where possible, and not hybrids, because the latter will not give predictable results, though you might come up with something interesting. If you've got one good species plant and it is isolated from similar species, you minimize the risk of hybridization and you should end up with a near copy of the parent. The seed heads normally indicate when they are ripe by changing colour from green to beige or brown, though there are some cases where immature seed gives better results than the mature kind. The best days to collect are when it

Fleshy fruits and berries

The seed that is wrapped up in a food parcel, e.g. a pear, that is meant to be eaten by an animal which deposits the seed through its faeces some distance from the parent, needs special treatment. You have to separate the seed from the soft, fleshy covering, and in the case of a rose hip, for example, that is easy enough. In autumn flick the seed out with the point of a sharp knife and put it in a clear plastic bag containing some coir, and keep for about 10 weeks at 21°C (70°F), before refrigerating in late winter for a further four weeks.

ABOVE Ornamental grass stems need to be kept in a cool, dry place for several days before the seeds are stripped off.

ABOVE Even the smallest seed heads can contain scores of tiny seeds. Collect the moment that they ripen.

ABOVE Inspect the seed carefully and, if it is damp, gently dry it on absorbent paper to avoid any risk of rotting.

ABOVE Rose hips, often resembling tiny tomatoes, are packed with fresh seed that needs to be stored in plastic bags with coir.

ABOVE Seed packets usually provide all the growing tips you need on the back; keep in a cool, dry place until ready for use.

ABOVE Keep a close check on the seed heads in the garden, and on their changing colours as they ripen from green to brown.

ABOVE The seeds in the purple, oval autumn fruit on *Callicarpa bodinieri* var. *giraldii* can be sown either fresh or dried.

ABOVE If you're not sure when a seedhead has ripened, keep a close watch and it will open when it is ready for the seed to be sown.

Attractive fruits and seedheads

Many plants provide attractive pods, seedheads or fruits. If you do not want to collect the following, leave the stems uncut with the pods or fruits hanging on.
- *Celastrus orbiculatus* Hermaphrodite Group – orange fruit splits open exposing red seed.
- Chocolate vine (*Akebia quinata*) – fruit turns from plump and green to violet-purple.
- Dead man's fingers (*Decaisnea fargesii*) – deep blue plump fruit.
- Foxglove tree (*Paulownia tomentosa*) – large, acorn-like capsules.
- Indian bean tree (*Catalpa bignonioides*) – slender brown pods up to 30cm (12in) long.
- *Iris foetidissima* – large capsules split to reveal orange-scarlet seed.
- Passion flower (*Passiflora*) – in a long, hot summer it produces egg-like fruit.

Ageing seed

When opening seed packets, there is sometimes far more seed than you could ever need. If you're not giving some away, or growing extra numbers to keep in reserve, simply take what you need and reseal the packet, keeping it in a dry, cool place. But for how long? Fresh seed usually gives the best, most consistent results. In general, you can try keeping vegetable seed for two years in an airtight container at a uniform temperature (but not parsnips – they do need to be grown from fresh seed). Flower seed might keep for slightly longer.

The undeniable fact, though, is that seed deteriorates as it ages, giving increasingly unpredictable results. One way to test this is by scattering some seed on damp kitchen paper and seeing how much of it germinates. If you're still unsure, use new packets of fresh seed to guarantee the best results, especially where you're creating a special feature rather than less obvious, distant gap-fillers.

is dry and fine, without gale force winds. This is not just for obvious, practical reasons but because wet seed can be prone to mould.

Drying seed

If the seed is wet, then dry it gently on kitchen paper but not with a vigorous blast from a hairdryer. Even if it is not wet, let it dry in labelled paper bags (never plastic ones or sealed containers that lead to a build up of humidity which creates mould and rotting) on a sunny windowsill. When storing capsules from the pea family, violas, and impatiens, etc., all of which ping open and can expel the seed right across a room, make sure that the tops of the bags are tied.

Storage

If you need to separate the seed from the chaff and other bits of plant by sieving or winnowing, put everything in an open box and then blow across the surface. The seed

then goes into a sealed envelope, in a cool, dark place, avoiding any humidity, but some kinds need to be refrigerated (mimicking a cold winter spell out in the wild), while others are what's called 'desiccation-intolerant' and need a container with a high moisture and oxygen content.

ABOVE The seed pods of *Lilium regale* are ready the moment the tops crack open; sow immediately or keep until early spring.

Sowing seed indoors

Getting the garden off to an early start usually means sowing seed indoors, where you can control the growing conditions. This is where it all starts. Stick to the rules and you will have more seedlings than you know what to do with.

Timing

There is sometimes a burst of early spring hot weather when it is very tempting to start sowing all your seeds, but be careful when doing this indoors. When the seedlings have shot up they will need to be pricked out and transferred to larger, individual pots, but if you do not have a greenhouse or cold frame you simply will not have enough windowsill space to line them up until it is safe to plant them outside, when both day and night temperatures are reliably warm. Some plants (for example courgettes) shoot up in days and can be left until mid- to late spring while others (chillies) take longer to germinate and need to be started off in early spring to give the first crop time to develop.

ABOVE Nicely spaced out seedlings in a propagating case. Do not completely remove the lid if you have cats because they will curl up on the compost and crush the seedlings.

Containers

Choosing the right container for the right seed is partly a matter of preference. Use seed trays for large numbers of plants that do not mind root disturbance, and sow the seed thinly and evenly to avoid getting concentrated packed clumps of seedlings that are hard to separate and prick out, when they need to be moved into larger containers. The best way to avoid that problem with the tiniest fine seed is to mix it with sand, and scatter it down the fold in a piece of paper. When growing large numbers of plants that dislike being disturbed, choose root trainers, large modules or builder's guttering with lots of holes drilled in the bottom to let the water drain out, sowing the seed at the final spacing. Using all three means you will avoid the task of potting on and the seedlings will be big enough to survive outside. When growing small numbers of plants, just four or five different chillies or tomato plants, for example, grow each variety in a 5cm (2in) wide plastic or biodegradable pot. Put two or three seeds in each pot, and remove the weakest to leave one strong seedling.

Compost (soil mix)

Either sow seed in seed compost, or multi-purpose compost that has been mixed with a handful of

ABOVE Tomatoes are usually sown about eight weeks before planting time in the first few weeks of summer.

ABOVE Chillies and sweet peppers need to be sown at 20°C (68°F) from late winter because they can take 30 days to germinate.

vermiculite or perlite. Fill to near the top of the container, and then level and lightly firm down the surface to eliminate any air pockets using a smooth piece of wood cut to size or the bottom of an empty pot or seed tray. When covering fine seed on the surface, either use sieved compost (soil mix) or vermiculite which lets both light and water penetrate. Water with a fine rose spray, turned upwards, or by standing the containers in pans of water where it will be absorbed by capillary action. To generate a warm, moist, humid atmosphere, put the small containers in a clear plastic bag in an airing cupboard, or without the bag in a propagator, usually at a consistent 18°C (65°F), and regularly wipe off the condensation. When the seedlings appear, remove the protective cover, and water as necessary, as before. Keep turning the containers in order to prevent the seedlings from growing at an angle toward the light.

Soil depths

The finer the seed, the closer it is planted to the surface, and the shallower the soil covering. The rule of thumb is that a seed should be covered by its own depth.

ABOVE *Rhodochiton atrosanguineus* makes prodigious growth from a spring sowing, and by the end of summer will easily cover a wall.

SOWING SEED IN A SEED TRAY

1 Fill the seed tray to near the top with compost (soil mix) and perlite, and then lightly tap it down to flatten the surface.

2 Sow the seed thinly and evenly across the surface. This gives much better results than packing the seed in tight clusters.

3 Then lightly cover tiny seed with a fine layer of compost, which can be sieved over to remove any grit and lumps.

4 Always add a clearly written label so you know what is in each seed tray, and stand in a pan of water, giving a thorough drink.

5 Carefully put the clear lid on top, having thoroughly cleaned it on both sides to ensure good light levels.

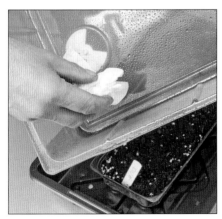

6 The moment you see any condensation on the inside of the lid, promptly remove it, wipe it off and then replace.

Pricking out

When the seedlings have opened their first pair of true leaves, not the small, rounded seed leaves (cotyledons), they can be pricked out. This is a vital step because the growing plant now needs more light, space and compost. Make sure that the compost (soil mix) is on the dry side, and then carefully fork out the seedlings, handling them very carefully by the leaves, avoiding the weak, easily damaged stems. The seedlings go straight into the next size pot, filled with multi-purpose compost, or modules (a 24-module tray is excellent for bedding plants). If putting them back into a seed tray, use fresh compost, and space them out about 36mm (1½in) apart. Make individual holes with a dibber, carefully lower the seedlings so that they are at the same depth as before, and firm in, before watering again with a fine spray turned upwards. If continuing to grow on a windowsill, keep turning the containers to get vertical growth. Seedlings are incredibly light sensitive and need regular attention.

Composts for permanent containers

If you are growing plants permanently in containers, you have a wide choice of composts (soil mixes). All have several pros and cons.

• Loam, or soil-based compost – the John Innes range is basically a recipe with No. 1 aimed at seeds and cuttings, No. 2 (with double the amount of nutrients) at young plants, and No. 3 (treble the amount) at greedy long-term plants (such as shrubs). However, the nutrients get used up and flushed out after about 12 weeks, at which point you will have to start adding a liquid feed. Some peat is included.

• Peat-free compost – the alternatives include green waste, coir, and composted bark (but not for seeds or seedlings). Green waste is made from recycled household waste, while coir is made from shredded coconut husks (imported mainly from Sri Lanka, stacking up plenty of air miles) and has few nutrients. Coir-based compost is mixed with two parts of loam-based, or multi-purpose, to one of the coir. Use for one-season displays but note that it dries out quickly and needs regular drinks. Ideally choose a bag containing a mixture of different organic materials.

• Peat-based (or loamless or soilless) compost, including the multi-purpose kind – again for one-season displays. It is lightweight but dries out quickly, and has low nutrient levels, although these can be easily supplemented.

• Ericaceous compost – essential for acid-loving plants.

Hardening off

Plants that have been raised in a sheltered, warm environment need to be acclimatized over several weeks to outside conditions before they are permanently grown in the garden. The longer they have been in the warmth, the longer they will need to be toughened up. If they go straight out they will probably suffer a significant check to their growth. The ideal place is a cold frame, but if you haven't got one, initially stand plants outside in a sheltered position with dappled light during the day, for example at the base of a hedge, avoiding any extremes, and bring them in at night, until the night-time temperatures start picking up and they can be left out

ABOVE Some different composts (soil mixes) and additives. Back row: multi-purpose compost, loam-based compost and moss peat. Front row: water retention granules, vermiculite and coarse grit.

ABOVE The ideal place to harden off young plants, and acclimatize them to outside temperatures, is in a cold frame. Regularly open the lid to provide good ventilation, but keep it closed and covered on cold nights.

for the occasional mild night until, finally, these temperatures are not in any danger of suddenly falling. Even if the plants have been hardened off, though, and there is suddenly a bad early summer with fierce, chilly winds, delay planting until the weather returns to normal. If you have got a cold frame, initially keep it closed at night, cover it with old carpet if the temperatures are set to dive, and open it on mild days to give plenty of ventilation.

Aftercare

After all this attention, don't just leave ornamental plants to themselves. Keep a close eye on their development and act promptly if they become lanky. Pinch out their growing tips to encourage more bushy growth from lower down. To create really bushy, prolific flowering plants (for example, fuchsias), you might need to keep pinching out this new emergent growth in early summer.

In addition, if young seedlings are grown with too much warmth and not enough light, you end up with weak, spindly, elongated growth, so keep an eye on these factors too.

PRICKING OUT SEEDLINGS

1 Occasionally, gently brush the tops of the seedlings to mimic the wind. This helps produce sturdier, more resilient plants.

2 When young seedlings develop their first pair of true leaves, not the initial rounded kind, they are ready to be given more space.

3 Carefully prise them out of the compost (soil mix), perhaps using a kitchen fork. Do not damage the roots or crush the leaves.

4 To make the new planting hole, use a pencil or dibber and carefully lower in the roots. They must be at the same depth as before. Water.

ABOVE Young plants can become rather lanky. To generate extra flowering branches, nip back the tops to force out more side growth.

ABOVE A bushy young fuchsia that has been regularly pinched out in the first few weeks of summer, giving a greater mass of flowers.

ABOVE Pelargoniums respond well to regular pinching out in late spring, and they quickly produce extra flowering growth for summer.

Sowing seed outdoors

To get good success rates, it is worth following the accepted way of sowing seed. If you just throw seed about the garden the odds are that little will germinate, and certainly not where you want it, standing only a poor chance of thriving.

Where and when to plant

The first key requirement is deciding whether you are sowing straight into a special nursery seed bed (later transplanting the seedlings, for example hardy biennials, to their final position), or whether you are sowing the plants exactly where they are to flower (for example hardy annuals). But note that *Gypsophila* and parsley, with deep, anchoring taproots, hate being lifted and disturbed. If you do it, you will check their growth.

Next, check whether you are growing hardy plants that can withstand frost and can therefore be sown when the soil temperature is above 9°C (48°F). Half-hardy plants can take the cold but cannot withstand actual frost, and need a temperature of 15–18°C (60–65°F), while tender plants cannot be sown or planted outside until late spring or early summer (though they can certainly be given an early start by germinating them indoors with the half-hardies). Hardy biennials are sown and planted in the summer, to stay outside all winter and flower the following year. When you are sowing seed where the plants are going to flower, do check their needs, finding out which require full sun, dappled light or shade, which require poor, dry, free-draining soil (at the one extreme) and which require moist, rich ground, with plenty of added organic matter (at the other) and which will give good results in average conditions. Grow the right plant in the right place, and it will thrive. Grow it in the wrong place, and it won't.

The soil

When sowing tiny seed, it needs to be sown in fine, crumbly soil that will let in light and air to help the seed germinate. Dig the ground

ABOVE Before sowing directly outside, mark out the areas for the different plants first, to organize the contrasting blocks of colour.

when the soil is dry because if it is wet and squishy you will badly compact it if you stand on it. One of the reasons for growing vegetables in narrow beds is precisely to avoid this problem. You should be able to keep your anchoring foot on the path and avoid damaging the soil texture. Also make sure every weed and its roots have been removed (far easier to get them out now than later), and then rake over the ground to get out any stones and to break up the soil. If there are any large clods, simply use your rake like a hammer and smash down on them, breaking them into tiny pieces. Poor soil can be given an all-purpose feed, lightly raked into the topsoil. You now need to eliminate any air pockets because if seeds fall into them, they will struggle. Do this by shuffling over the ground to flatten the soil surface, but do not stamp on it. Rake over it again, giving a crumbly soil topping to a depth of 5cm (2in) and you're ready to sow.

ABOVE Everyone wants a garden full of wildlife, but that does not include household pets. Covering these emerging sweet pea plants with netting will help keep off cats and dogs looking for a toilet, and clearly indicates to garden visitors that they must keep clear of the fragile growth.

SOWING SEED OUTDOORS 41

Lines or drifts

Before sowing, you need to decide whether to scatter the seed in all directions over the area (called broadcast sowing, which is how you sow a lawn), or in neat, precise, well-spaced straight rows. If you are sowing a patch of annuals, then the broadcast method is best so that you get natural and irregular-looking blocks of plants. To mark out an informal area, define it with a stick, leaving lines in the soil, rubbing them out if you make mistakes. If you are creating a more structured, geometric layout then use canes and string to create straight divisions.

When you are happy with the different areas, clearly mark out the boundaries using sand poured out of an old, dry plastic water-bottle.

Sowing

Broadcast the seed on a still day, giving an even covering, always holding some seed back as gap fillers, then lightly rake over so that the seed is not exposed on the surface, label and water (or water before sowing).

RIGHT When planning and sowing a vegetable garden, always think about the range of colours, shapes and heights that will create an attractive, imaginative look.

SOWING SEED IN AN OUTDOOR BED

1 Give the bed a thorough weed, also getting out stones and breaking up any clods by smashing down on them with a fork.

2 Then rake the soil thoroughly lengthwise and crosswise to give a flat, even surface with a loose, crumbly top.

3 Next, mark out the areas for the different plants using a stick. Check that the final look will work from all sides.

4 When you are happy with the final divisions, clearly mark them out using an old bottle filled with dry sand.

5 Scatter the seed over the surface, giving an even spread, though any cluttered seedlings can be thinned out later.

6 Finally cover the entire area with netting in order to keep off hungry pigeons, and household pets and children. Water.

Thinning

Though it might seem an advantage to have huge numbers of plants packed together, you really are better off having slightly fewer, stronger, healthier, more vigorous, better fed, better performing plants than a large number growing so close together that they are fighting over food and water, struggling in periods of drought, and prone to disease. More is definitely less.

THINNING PLANTS

ABOVE Keep a close eye on the emerging seedlings, and when you see a few growing too close together, pull out the weakest.

Weeding

Keep an eye out for weeds, and get rid of them the moment they appear. That is obviously easier when growing plants in straight rows because you can spot a rogue seedling and easily whip it out, or just run the hoe between the rows and leave the upended weed seedlings to shrivel in the sun.

Watering

Also make sure that the seedlings get nicely watered on a regular basis when the ground is dry, though as the roots get longer aim for a good watering every 10 days or so to encourage them to tunnel down deep for moisture. If you pamper the plants and keep the topsoil moist, then the roots will happily stay in the top layer, and the plants will quickly suffer in dry periods because this layer dries out quickest, meaning you have to keep running outside to supply more water. Do not get locked in that cycle. Also note that when giving established plants a good drink it takes a huge amount of water to soak even several inches into the ground. Check by putting a trowel in the soil to see how deep the water has sunk. Also, never water on a hot day because a huge percentage of the water is promptly lost through evaporation. The plants only get a brief drink. Do it last thing at night and the plants have got a good 10 hours to drink. You will immediately notice how much sturdier they look in the morning. To stop lawns from getting brown and patchy, do not keep cropping the grass too severely, but let it grow quite long, resulting in longer roots that go deeper down for a drink.

If there is a water restriction in your area, investigate different ways of using rain run-off channelled into water butts and concentrate on drought-resistant plants, for example growing sweet corn and pumpkins in the vegetable garden.

Keeping out the pests

Put netting over any seedlings where possible, because inquisitive birds can rip them out in seconds. Look out of the window early in the morning and you will see pigeons and crows staggering around the

ABOVE Annual cosmos can be sown directly outside in late spring, and is one of the main ingredients of cottage garden displays.

ABOVE A seed-raised bergenia injecting a colourful touch in spring. Grow it in full sun or light, partial shade.

ABOVE The larger sunflowers produce enormous flowers, nearly 25cm (10in) wide, so avoid growing them in packed clumps.

Stopping slugs

The only foolproof method of stopping slugs from demolishing your seedlings is to stand guard at night – and that's right through the night – and pick them off by hand, unless you want to use large quantities of toxic slug pellets. There are countless other methods of controlling slugs, which can be effective. These include: scattering eggshells or sharp sand over the ground; using saucers or jam jars filled with beer to drown them (sunk into the soil near valuable plants); using upturned grapefruit halves as traps, because slugs love the pith; stretching out lengths of copper slug tape as a barrier; and watering nematodes into the soil – these then seek out and destroy slugs underground (recent research suggests the killing ingredient might actually be a bacterium carried by the nematodes), which also means that older slugs which live on the surface are relatively safe.

Try eliminating slugs' hiding places, for example old pots left lying around the garden, or damp, dark places where slugs congregate. Provided you are not trying to poison them, keep a pond well-stocked with frogs, who slurp slugs down as a delicacy, and encourage thrushes, hedgehogs and ground beetles, which also like haute cuisine.

ABOVE Keep a lookout for slugs in cool, damp conditions, or plants with young soft succulent stems will become a prime target.

Herbaceous plants that are less prone to slug damage

Acanthus mollis
Alchemilla
Bergenia
Dicentra spectabilis
Eryngium
Gaillardia
Hemerocallis
Papaver orientale
Pulmonaria

garden pecking at everything and anything, even if you have scarecrows. Netting should also keep out dogs and cats, and there are ultrasound devices to scare off the latter (that necessitate erecting speakers), although many cats ignore them. Netting, erected over canes firmly fixed in the soil, is also vital if you have young children as a way of telling them and their friends that this is definitely a no-go area.

ABOVE Hostas are prone to slug and snail damage, and are often grown in raised pots topped by gravel to avoid any damage.

ABOVE Annual mallows (*Lavatera*) can be sown outside from mid-spring, and give a long flowery show through the summer.

ABOVE Whenever you have a spare patch of ground to the front of a border, grow richly scented stock (*Matthiola longipetala*) from seed.

ABOVE Love-in-a-mist (*Nigella*) can be sown directly outside either in mid-spring or several months before, in autumn.

Cuttings

If growing plants from seed involves a huge leap of faith (will they/won't they grow?), with cuttings you are halfway there. The job is usually incredibly simple: you just snip off a length of growth and plant it up. There are ideal times to do this, but you can, if desperate, do it at other times, although your chances of success will be lower.

The key point is not rushing the young plants-from-cuttings into the garden, because they can quickly get lost among larger, more vigorous plants, getting shaded and smothered – suddenly, at the end of autumn, you cannot find them. If you have a cold frame or nursery bed, put the young plants in there, giving them time to put on growth. The larger they are when planted out, the better they will be at coping with any extremes, including spells without decent rain and winter nights when the temperatures dive. Cared-for cuttings give the best results, so make sure they are not ignored.

This chapter begins by looking at cuttings basics, tackling everything from the best time to take cuttings, how you take them and the rooting process to raising cuttings in pots. It then moves on to the different kinds of cuttings – greenwood, semi-ripe, and hardwood – and even those that can be taken from leaves and roots. The chapter finishes with four special features on taking rose, conifer, heather and willow cuttings.

LEFT A large reddish-purple *Buddleja davidii* 'Dartmoor' grown from a summer cutting, attracting large numbers of butterflies.

Cuttings basics

You can take cuttings of tips, stems, leaves and roots at various stages throughout the growing season, starting off with the youngest, freshest growth at the plant's tip, usually taken in spring. Once you realize what each cutting needs in order to succeed, it is actually a simple job getting high success rates.

The best growth

Look for a healthy, sturdy, non-flowering shoot (from this year's new, quick growth), which will have better growth potential than a shoot with buds or flowers. If you have a choice of plants from which to take the cutting, select the best, because you're producing a copy. Further, if the parent is now an old, relatively unproductive plant, nip it back one year before. This will generate a fresh batch of better shoots to be used as cuttings.

Timing

Ideally, take cuttings first thing in the morning when the stems are full of water. If doing this later in the day, do not under any circumstances

ABOVE All cotoneasters are easily grown from cuttings, taken from spring to autumn. The showiest kinds make substantial unfussy shrubs or trees with an abundance of berries loved by birds. Others can be used as ground cover or weeping standards.

leave them lying around to wilt in the hot sun. Get them potted up as quickly as possible. They should be about 10cm (4in) long without too much leafy growth. If there is too much foliage there is a danger that the cutting will lose more water than it can take up, making it wilt. It is sometimes advisable to trim off the top halves of the leaves.

Basic principles

The main principles that apply to the different types of cuttings in this chapter – greenwood, semi-ripe and hardwood – are shown here in the step sequences 'Taking tip cuttings from a ficus' (opposite) and 'Taking internodal cuttings from a fuchsia' (overleaf).

When taking the cuttings (e.g. the new young growth from the end of a stem), make the cut just above a leaf node. This means that the parent plant will not be left with an unproductive length of stem that will die back.

If using a side shoot, gently tug it away from the parent so that it retains a 'heel', or sliver of bark at the base. Then remove the lower leaves (give them a quick pull down), so that they do not come in contact with the compost (soil mix) and possibly rot.

The base of each cutting now needs to be trimmed to just below a node. This is crucial because that is exactly where the plant has the greatest potential for new root

ABOVE *Abelia grandiflora* can be easily grown from cuttings, especially if it is rooted in a heated propagator. It should take 1–2 years to flower, and makes a substantial shrub 3 x 4m (10 x 12ft). It is not totally hardy and needs to be planted in a sheltered position.

growth. Plants that do not root easily (and there are not that many) can be given a kick-start by lightly dabbing the end of the cutting in rooting powder. Too much will be counter-productive. The sooner the roots develop, the sooner the cutting will turn into an independent plant.

Internodal cuttings

The preceding cuttings rely on nodes, which means that each length of stem used as a cutting has one node at the base with more at the top. The base node generates all the root growth. But some plants can be grown from lengths of cutting that do not have a node at the base. The bottom cut is therefore made above a node, and often the entire length of the internodal stem produces roots. The advantage is that the stems produce more cuttings than normal.

Potting up

While the cuttings are developing, they are entirely reliant on you. Use an open-textured seed or cuttings compost (soil mix), which has just the right amount of nutrients. Insert approximately three around the edge of an 8cm (3in) plastic pot, and carefully firm in, making sure that the bare 'leg' of each is in contact

ABOVE Shrubby and perennial St. John's wort (*Hypericum*) can be grown from cuttings, and normally takes 3–6 weeks to root.

TAKING TIP CUTTINGS FROM A FICUS

1 To propagate a new *Ficus*, take a leafy cutting in spring that is about 10cm (4in) long, cutting if off just above a node.

2 Then trim the cutting, making this second cut just below a node, and discard the redundant bottom length.

3 Remove the lower leaves. If too many are left the cutting will lose more moisture through the foliage than it can drink up.

4 Arrange the cuttings in seed or cuttings compost (soil mix), spacing them out equidistantly around the edge of the pot.

5 Water and add a clear plastic covering to keep the cuttings warm and humid, but wipe off any condensation when it appears.

Gardenias

Since gardenias can be expensive, they are worth propagating by cuttings. They root within eight weeks.

with compost (soil mix) and not an air pocket. Then water using a fine rose spray, because if you pour straight from the spout of a watering can you will compress the compost. To ensure that the cuttings go into a warm, humid environment, the pot either needs to go in a heated propagator or be sealed in a clear plastic bag – kept clear of the cuttings by short, vertical canes – and held in place with a rubber band until all have rooted. Periodically wipe off any condensation. With firmer cuttings, for example a pelargonium, the bag is not so necessary.

Aftercare

When young cuttings start putting on new growth, they can be taken out of this 'hot house' and potted up individually. It is vital that they are not put under any stress. Avoid extremes of direct sun and permanent shade, giving them a bright, cool place in a greenhouse or on a windowsill. Keep turning them to avoid the stem angling exclusively in one direction to the light.

ABOVE The rather shrubby busy Lizzie (*Impatiens walleriana*) can be grown from spring cuttings, then treated as an annual.

ABOVE The climbing honeysuckle (*Lonicera*) quickly roots in four weeks. Look for sound, vigorous cuttings that are 5cm (2in) long.

LEFT Every garden needs at least one mock orange (*Philadelphus*) for its rich summer scent. It is easily propagated by cuttings.

TAKING INTERNODAL CUTTINGS FROM A FUCHSIA

1 During the growing season, choose a strong, vigorous, healthy shoot from a fuchsia, with several pairs of leaves.

2 Using a clean, sharp knife, make cuts just above each pair of leaves. Hold the stem very carefully to avoid accidental damage.

3 The bottom piece of stem is left on and not trimmed off as for tip cuttings, because rooting will occur right along its length.

The range of cuttings

Once you understand how tip cuttings are taken and grow, it's time to look at three more kinds. The main distinction between greenwood, semi-ripe and hardwood cuttings is the time when they are taken. Greenwood, as the name implies, means that the new young growth is still green and fresh and has not hardened and become brown and woody. Semi-ripe means that the growth is gradually maturing, and hardwood means that the cuttings can be taken later in the season when the growth has toughened up. All are dealt with on the following pages.

Plants grown from internodal cuttings	
Clematis	Hydrangea
Fuchsia	Hypericum
Hedera	Verbena

RIGHT If you have a favourite fuchsia, keep nipping off the growing points when it is young, to create a bushy plant. The following year, use the new shoots as cuttings, creating an even more impressive display.

ABOVE Clematis cuttings are taken from spring to midsummer when the plants are in full growth.

ABOVE Ivy (Hedera) is one of the easiest climbers to propagate by cuttings, but keep the cuttings out of damaging direct sun.

ABOVE Lavender cuttings can be delayed until after flowering; nip off the top growth in spring to encourage more shoots.

Greenwood cuttings

Outdoor plants generate new shoots in early summer, and the tips of this new growth can be used to make greenwood cuttings. They are easier to handle than those taken from spring growth, and less likely to wilt.

Timing

You can basically take cuttings throughout the growing season, the only difference being the degree to which the stems have aged and hardened, and their speed of growth. This will vary from plant to plant, and since the differences between softwood, greenwood and semi-ripe cuttings is not that radical, the most important factor is when you can do the best possible job. Far better to take a mid- or late season cutting when you can tend it well than an early season one that is going to get ignored and perform poorly.

Greenwood cuttings are an in-between, early summer stage, being taken after the tip and softwood kind but before the semi-ripe. Close examination shows a slight difference in texture and colour, and while the rooting takes slightly

ABOVE Elder (*Sambucus*) roots easily from cuttings from spring on, with the pots being stood outside in dappled shade.

longer than the tip cuttings, the stem will be that bit firmer and more mature. Again, it is sensible to take a few extras in case of failure.

Taking cuttings

As with the tip or softwood kind, take the cuttings early in the morning, when the stems are still full of moisture. They should be trimmed to about 10cm (4in) long, just below a node to maximize the chances of successful rooting. Give the leaves on the bottom third of the stem a quick pull down to get rid of them, and if there is plenty of leaf growth, cut it in half, crosswise. If a large, full head of leaves is left on, there is a danger that the plant will wilt as transpiration of moisture exceeds the take-up rate, causing cell damage. The snag left on the parent plant needs to be cut back to just above a node, where new branching will occur. By nipping off this growing end, the parent plant will respond by activating its reserve supply of latent or dormant buds, which is why most trees, for example, react so energetically when they are coppiced, firing out a spray of new growth in all directions.

ABOVE If you need a box hedge or more topiary specimens, then use the early summer trimmings to raise new plants.

ABOVE Gardens cannot have enough richly scented daphnes, and numbers can be increased by taking greenwood cuttings.

ABOVE Grow extra pyracanthas from cuttings to make a robust, spiny hedge packed with brightly coloured berries in autumn.

ABOVE When taking magnolia cuttings, you can help them root by making a light wound at the base of the stem.

Potting up

The cuttings need to be potted up in seed or cuttings compost (soil mix), around three per 8cm (3in) pot. Do not firm the soil down too much because you want a light, open, free-draining texture conducive to good root spread. Water the cuttings in using a fine rose spray, and then place the pot in a warm, humid environment, best provided by a heated propagator or sealed, clear plastic bag. Make sure that it is well supported at the top by short canes so that it does not touch the leaves, and seal it with a rubber band around the base of the pot.

Aftercare

Keep the cuttings in a bright, cool place where there is no danger of wilting or being stuck in the shade. When they start developing, pot them up individually, and keep turning them to avoid angled growth toward the light. However, they cannot go permanently outside at this stage. Gradually harden them off by standing them in a cold frame when the weather has warmed up. For the first few cold nights, bring them indoors. Thereafter cover the lid with old carpet on frosty nights, removing this in the daytime.

Sports

A plant with all-green leaves might suddenly and unpredictably develop a shoot, for example, with attractive variegated foliage. Such a sport, as it is called, is caused by a random genetic mutation, and if you want to propagate this shoot, do so by taking cuttings. When a sport is unstable it can suddenly revert to its all-green state. Quickly remove any branch without the variegated leaves or, in time, the whole plant will be affected.

TAKING GREENWOOD CUTTINGS FROM A KALANCHOE

1 Carefully check the parent plant, looking for likely non-flowering cuttings with firm, vigorous growth and healthy leaves.

2 Take a cutting by slicing straight across the stem with a clean, sharp knife. Do not squeeze and bruise the tissue.

3 Trim the cutting, first getting rid of the largest leaves, and then to leave the shoot about 5cm (2in) long.

4 Hold the cutting by the edge of a leaf, making sure that you do not damage it, and dip it in a rooting/fungicide compound.

5 Now insert it in an 8cm (3in) pot that has been filled with free-draining compost (soil mix) with plenty of added grit. Water.

6 Finally, place a clear, clean plastic dome on top to provide a warm, humid environment. Clean off any condensation.

Semi-ripe cuttings

If you missed the chance to take cuttings earlier in the spring or summer, or suddenly realize that you need more of a particular plant for next year, it is not a tragedy. Semi-ripe cuttings can be taken now, in late summer.

Taking cuttings in late summer

Many deciduous plants are best propagated now, when the new growth has lost its soft, sappy look, and is turning brown and woody though still slightly pliable. Take 15cm (6in) long cuttings, removing them just above a node on the parent plant, and then trim them just below a node. Or, if using side growth, gently tear it away from the parent so that it is left with a 'heel' of old bark at the base. Semi-ripe cuttings, being more mature than softwood ones, have a higher success rate.

Stripping and rooting

The base leaves now need to be removed, being given a quick pull down, so that the bottom third to half of the cutting is clear. You can also nick the base with a knife to remove a piece of bark and expose the growth cells in the cambium to help generate roots. Tricky plants can have the end dipped in rooting

ABOVE Cuttings of the Californian lilac (*Ceanothus*) are best taken with a 'heel', a sliver of bark at the base, to help rooting.

TAKING SEMI-RIPE CUTTINGS FROM A WEIGELA

1 Weigelas root easily and quickly from cuttings, taking about four weeks. Take the cutting just above a node.

2 Next, trim the cutting just below a node and remove the lower leaves so that none are left in contact with the soil to rot.

3 Insert them in open, free-draining soil with plenty of added grit in a cold frame, and then firm down to eliminate any air pockets.

4 The finished cuttings, each with an array of leaves, look like this. They are well spaced out, giving them plenty of room to grow.

5 Finish off by gently watering in with an upturned rose spray in order to avoid dislodging the cuttings.

Plants propagated as semi-ripe cuttings

Argyranthemum
Berberis thunbergii
Ceanothus
Cistus
Deutzia
Elaeagnus
Forsythia
Pyracantha
Rubus
Salvia officinalis cultivars
Senecio maritima
Weigela

ABOVE One of the most valuable garden shrubs, a berberis can be propagated by taking semi-ripe cuttings in late summer. To get the best autumn leaf colours and an excellent show of fruit, grow it in full sun. Many make very effective dense hedges.

ABOVE Forsythias are versatile plants, making useful shrubs and hedges. Cuttings can be taken from spring to autumn.

Rock roses

Mediterranean rock roses are not reliably hardy, so if you live in a region where you cannot guarantee mild winter temperatures, it is best to take cuttings in case you suddenly lose an impressive plant. Give the new shrub a sheltered hot spot and good drainage.

and they will root well. Remove any fallen leaves, keep the glass free of condensation and cover the frame with old carpet when the temperature dives. Either plant them out at the end of spring or wait until the following autumn. Alternatively, provide warmth and humidity by inserting the pot in a heated propagator or inside a clear plastic

bag. Insert short vertical canes to lift the bag clear of the cuttings, and seal around the base with a rubber band. When the cuttings have clearly rooted, they should be individually potted up and kept in a greenhouse or cold frame over winter.

Aftercare

The following spring, after the last of the frosts, they can be hardened off by placing them in a cold frame before planting out in autumn.

powder, and then be given a light tap to get rid of any excess. Do not apply too much, thinking that it will apply a late-season push because it will have the opposite effect.

Potting up

Arrange the cuttings around the edge of a pot, firming them into cutting or all-purpose compost (soil mix) with added sharp sand to improve the drainage. Water in using a fine rose spray, and nip off the tops if they are very sappy. You can then put the potted cuttings straight in a cold frame, giving them plenty of ventilation on mild days,

ABOVE The spring- and summer-flowering deutzias make excellent border shrubs, with extra plants being raised from cuttings.

ABOVE The rock rose (*Cistus*) tends to be short-lived so periodically take semi-ripe cuttings to guarantee you have replacements.

Hardwood cuttings

You can successfully take cuttings in autumn, when the leaves have fallen, from many deciduous trees and shrubs. They require little effort, though they will not be ready for planting out for possibly one year.

Deciduous trees and shrubs

The best time to propagate such plants is in the second half of autumn, as the leaves are falling, into early winter, though if you miss this period you can still take them through to the start of spring, through the dormant period. This particularly applies to willows (*Salix*) and poplars (*Populus*). Evergreens are best taken in autumn. Of all the cuttings methods discussed, hardwood cuttings are the most trouble-free kind, partly because the stems have sufficient food reserves to generate sturdy root growth, and partly because they require only a pair of secateurs, one spade and a small, spare piece of well-weeded land that you will not need for 12 months.

ABOVE Evaluate the garden at the end of summer and, if you need more topiary, there will still be time to take box cuttings.

ABOVE Elder (*Sambucus*) cuttings, taken with a 'heel', usually give very good results but avoid pithy shoots that tend to rot.

Making the cut

In general, aim for a 15–20cm (6–8in) length of ripe stem that has developed this current year. It will be hard, woody and darker than the softwood kind, will not be pliable, and needs to be pencil thick. Make a straight cut at the base of the cutting, just below a node. Then trim the soft tip, making an angled cut just above a node. Making the one straight and one angled cut immediately indicates which is the top and bottom, should you forget. If you are growing a tree, do not remove the top, but leave the cutting intact to produce a clean, straight trunk. Finally, strip the leaves off the bottom two-thirds of evergreens.

Rooting

Dip the bottom ends in rooting powder. Trickier subjects might need to have the bottom sliver of wood nicked and lifted to expose the growth cells in the cambium. To plant them out, you need to make a simple trench by thrusting the spade into the ground, then pushing it slightly back to create a V shape but with one straight, vertical side. Move it to and fro a few times to make it work. Then pour in sharp sand to line the base to improve aeration and drainage. Insert the stems of shrubs, bottom first and 15cm (6in) apart, into the trench. Leave just the top third exposed, with trees going slightly deeper, just having the top bud showing. Then backfill and firm in, giving the cuttings a good drink.

ABOVE Extra numbers of buddlejas can raised at the end of the season, into the start of autumn. In the garden *Buddleja davidii* can be given a hard spring pruning, back to 30cm (12in) from the base. Less drastic pruning produces taller, less vigorous growth.

The best site

Make sure that the site is in full sun, and that the soil is free draining. To reduce the amount of time spent weeding and watering, try covering the length of the trench with landscaping fabric, and make planting slits in it. The weeds are thwarted by the lack of light, and the plastic acts as a mulch, reducing evaporation from the ground. If the only patch of ground you can spare has heavy clay soil, dig it up in advance, adding plenty of horticultural grit or sharp sand and mushroom compost to improve the structure and drainage. If you cannot use the garden, or you live in a particularly cold, exposed area, then set the cuttings in pots in a cold frame. Avoid using a warm greenhouse or there will be more premature top growth than root growth.

Aftercare

Keep the site weed free, and water in dry spells. Rooting will commence next spring when the temperatures rise, with the plants being transplanted the following autumn. If the cuttings are raised in a greenhouse and given gentle bottom heat, the process is much quicker, with a decent set of roots appearing by early spring.

Plants providing hardwood cuttings

Buddleja
Buxus
Clematis montana
Cornus
Deutzia scabra
Lonicera fragrantissima
Philadelphus
Populus
Ribes
Rubus
Salix
Sambucus
Symphoricarpos
Tamarix
Weigela

TAKING HARDWOOD CUTTINGS FROM A BUDDLEJA

1 Snip off a length of this year's growth from late autumn to winter, when most of the leaves have fallen.

2 Each individual cutting needs to be about 18cm (7in) long. If the tip has not hardened, snip it off. Remove any side shoots.

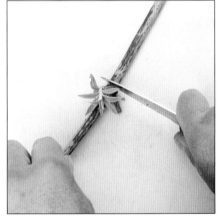
3 Trim the bottom cut just below a node, giving it a horizontal cut so that this end (which will be buried) is clearly marked.

4 Then nip off any growth at the base, because once planted it will simply rot. This will also encourage roots to develop.

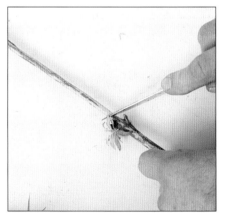
5 Then make a slanting cut just above a node at the top, which will clearly signify where all the top growth will emerge.

6 Finally, insert each cutting in a 15cm (6in) deep hole lined with sharp sand to improve drainage, firm in and water.

Leaf petiole and lateral vein-leaf cuttings

Plants that do not produce stems can be propagated from their leaves. There are two ways of doing this, and both are relatively quick and easy: from the leaf and stalk (or petiole), and from the leaf veins. Rooted plants should be ready for potting up after about two months.

Leaf petiole cuttings

The starting point is one leaf and its stalk (the petiole), typically taken from an African violet (*Saintpaulia*) in late spring or early summer. The new growth – shoots and roots – will appear around the base of the petiole.

Potting and rooting

Take cuttings carefully, slicing off the stalk-cum-leaf with a clean, sharp knife, and note the sharpness is very important. A scalpel is ideal. Then trim the end of the stalk to leave about 4cm (1½ in). Dip the end in rooting powder, blow off any excess, and then fill a seed tray with cuttings compost (soil mix). Make a series of small holes, well spaced apart, and then start inserting each stalk, but do so at a slight angle, angling them back at about 60 degrees, to avoid shading.

ABOVE Begonias can be propagated in various ways, by division, seed, stem cuttings and leaf petiole cuttings. When inserting the stalk, make sure that the leaf is resting on the surface. Begonias give a very impressive show indoors or in the conservatory.

TAKING LEAF PETIOLE CUTTINGS FROM A SAINTPAULIA

1 Always start with a healthy parent that has been well cared for, and look for three rich green, nicely rounded leaves.

2 Carefully slice them off using a razor-sharp blade, and then horizontally trim the stalk to a length of 4cm (1½ in).

3 Finally, insert the stalks equidistantly, making sure that they are angled at 60 degrees, with the leaf touching the surface.

Plants for leaf propagation

Begonia (petiole)
Gesneria (midrib)
Gloxinia (midrib)
Peperomia (petiole)
Ramonda (petiole)
Saintpaulia (petiole)
Sinningia (midrib)
Streptocarpus (midrib)

Aftercare

Then water in using a fine rose spray, after which the cuttings need high humidity to avoid any drying out. This is best provided in a heated propagator, at just over 19°C (66°F), or place in a clear plastic bag in a warm, bright place, but out of direct sun, or the temperature in the bag could quickly soar to damaging levels. Check that the cuttings are still at the correct angle so that they do not shade or cramp each other. In approximately six or seven weeks you should see the new growth starting to appear above the compost (soil mix). Remove the seed tray from the humid environment to avoid the onset of rot and, when the cuttings are large enough to be handled, transplant into individual pots.

TAKING LATERAL VEIN-LEAF CUTTINGS FROM A STREPTOCARPUS

1 Look for a shapely, well-developed leaf without any blemishes, and cut it cleanly off at the base.

2 Slice it neatly into horizontal sections, but maintain the original shape so that you immediately know which are the tops.

3 Plant them with the bottom end going in the compost (soil mix). They need to go in at a depth that will keep them upright.

4 Firm in and water, and then slide the container inside a clear plastic bag or propagator to maintain good humidity.

Lateral vein-leaf cuttings

This technique is extremely useful for plants with one long central vein and involves dividing it into horizontal sections, and is often carried out on a *Streptocarpus*. The leaves have the ability to produce young plants from their severed veins. Make sure you select a healthy green leaf with no defects, and then start slicing (again with a scalpel to give clean, straight cuts), producing sections never wider than 5cm (2in).

Potting and rooting

Do not forget which is the top edge because the sections are now planted up, with the bottom edges fitting into a narrow slit or trench in the compost. The sections must stand upright, with the bottom 12mm (½in) being buried, the top exposed to the air.

Aftercare

Place the seed tray in a warm, humid, bright environment (a clear plastic bag or a heated propagator), out of direct sun. The new, young growth should appear in about six weeks, when the seed tray can be removed from its humid environment. When the plants are large enough to be handled, they can be moved into their individual containers.

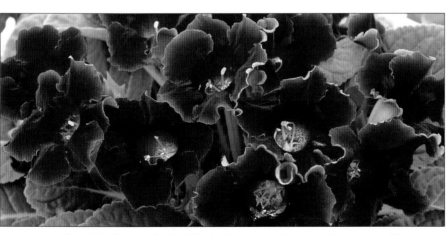

ABOVE A purple-pinkish florist's gloxinia (*Sinningia speciosa*), from Brazil, makes a striking houseplant with flaring, trumpet-shaped flowers in a range of bright colours. The large, velvety leaves have short, dense hairs. Keep it on the dry side over winter.

Leaf sections and midrib cuttings

Short for monocotyledons, monocots are partly distinguished because they often have clearly visible parallel lines on the surface of the leaves. They can be sliced into sections to grow large numbers of new plants. For dicotyledons, take midrib cuttings using the two long halves of a leaf.

Monocot leaf sections

Look for a long, healthy, blemish-free leaf, for example on a mother-in-law's tongue (*Sansevieria*), and cut it off at the base. Leaf sections are certainly quicker to produce new plants of the *Sansevieria* than seed or offsets, though strangely they may not inherit the parent's variegation. Lie the leaf face down and cut firmly and cleanly across it to produce 2.5cm (1in) wide slices. It is vital that you do not mix them up, as you need to remember which is the top edge.

Planting

Set the leaf sections out in rows in cuttings compost (soil mix), wedging them in bottom edge down so that the top edge is exposed to the air. Water with a fine rose spray. To avoid drying out, place the seed tray in a heated propagator at 21°C (70°F), or in a sealed, clear plastic bag, and give it light but not direct

ABOVE The pineapple flower (*Eucomis*) from South Africa can be propagated by slicing a leaf horizontally into separate sections.

TAKING LEAF SECTIONS FROM A SANSEVIERIA

1 Only take sections from a thriving, vigorous parent packed with leafy growth. Single out one new, well-formed, undamaged leaf.

2 Cut if off cleanly at the base, using a sharp knife, taking care not to squeeze or damage it in the process.

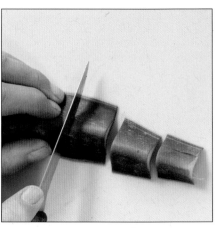

3 Lay it on a clean surface, so that is face down, and then proceed to slice it across the stem into equal sections.

4 You should now be left with a jigsaw arrangement of pieces, clearly showing the tops and bottoms of each piece.

5 Now plant them vertically in mini trenches, making sure that you insert the bottoms in the compost (soil mix) and not the tops.

Plants for propagating by leaf sections

Eucomis (monocot)
Galanthus (monocot)
Gesneria (midrib)
Gloxinia (midrib)
Heloniopsis (monocot)
Hyacinthoides (monocot)
Hyacinthus (monocot)
Lachenalia (monocot)
Leucojum (monocot)
Scilla (monocot)
Sinningia (midrib)
Streptocarpus (midrib)

TAKING MIDRIB CUTTINGS FROM A STREPTOCARPUS

1 Select a fully grown, healthy *Streptocarpus*, and cleanly sever an undamaged leaf at the base of the plant.

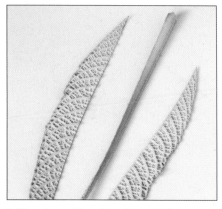

2 Slice along either side of the midrib, so that it can be removed, leaving the two whole side portions.

3 These are now planted lengthways with the edges that were closest to the midrib being inserted in the compost (soil mix).

sun to avoid a sudden escalation of the temperature. After approximately eight weeks new growth should have appeared, and the seed tray can be removed from its enclosed environment. When the young plants are large enough to handle, they can be moved to their individual containers.

Midrib cuttings

Dicotyledons usually have leaves with a midrib. Run a scalpel up one side of the central vein, and then the other, so that it can be removed and discarded.

Potting up

The two halves are then wedged in the compost, with the severed edges going into the mini trenches. Firm in and water. Again, a warm, humid environment is vital.

Aftercare

After approximately eight weeks, you will see new growth appearing along the base of the leaves, at which point the seed tray can be removed from its hot house. Separate the young plants, and move to their own individual containers.

Monocotyledons

Angiosperms – plants with seeds inside an ovary – have two divisions: monocotyledons and dicotyledons. The former have only one seed leaf (called a 'cotyledon'), parallel leaf veins, the absence of cambium and woody tissue, and therefore woody stems, and petals and sepals that are virtually identical. The latter have two seed leaves and cambium, producing thicker (possibly woody) stems. Also, their petals are generally arranged in fours or fives, while those of a monocotyledon appear in threes.

ABOVE Hyacinths can easily be propagated by leaf sections, giving extra scented plants for a spring display.

ABOVE The snowflake (*Leucojum*) is best in groups for a strong spring display, with new plants being raised by leaf sections.

ABOVE Scillas are bulbous perennials giving a gentle spring show, and are available in colours from white to blue and pink.

Leaf squares and leaf slashing

These two techniques are usually reserved for plants with large leaves, and they give good results producing a large batch of new plants from just one leaf, so that the parent plant will not suffer too much.

Leaf squares

Use any plant that has the means to generate new plants from its leaves, and begin by removing one whole, unblemished leaf. The larger the leaf, the greater the number of offspring. Promptly get rid of the leaf stalk, which is not needed, and then lay the leaf face down. Use a new clean scalpel (cleanliness is very important since this technique can result in rotting), and slice up the leaf into small squares, with the sides approximately 2cm (¾in) long. Each square must contain a piece of main vein. Leave them on the surface so that you remember which edge is nearest the base of the leaf.

Planting leaf squares

Get the seed tray ready, and fill with cuttings compost (soil mix). The surface needs to be flat but not compressed and squashed down hard. You then have two choices. Either lay the individual squares down on moist cuttings compost in rows, face

ABOVE *Begonia rex*, with its richly coloured large leaves, is a prime candidate for propagation by leaf squares.

up, pinned down by short lengths of bent wire, leaving 12mm (½in) between each, or, in the case of crinkled, wrinkled leaves that are impossible to lay flat giving good all-over surface contact, plant them vertically. Note that the end nearest the base of the leaf just goes into the compost, with the top end being exposed to the air. Do not bury them too deeply. The aim is simply to get them to stand upright. After watering with a fine rose spray, put the seed tray inside a clear plastic bag to create humidity at a temperature of about 21°C (70°F). Keep it out of direct sun, then wait approximately two months for the new growth to appear. Finally, remove from its humid bag and, when the cuttings are large enough to handle, after a few more weeks, they can be removed and individually potted up.

Leaf slashing

Best reserved for leaves with an all-over network of veins rather than those with one strong, dominant vein running up the length of the leaf, with laterals breaking from it, this simply involves making slashes in the leaf rather than cutting it up into segments.

SLICING LEAF SQUARES FROM A BEGONIA

1 Select a large, unblemished leaf, and remove it by making a quick, clean cut at the base of the stalk.

2 Next, trim off the stalk just below the leaf, taking care to lay it flat so that it is not bruised or damaged.

3 Using a clean sharp scalpel, remove several squares from the leaf, making sure that each one contains a piece of main vein.

4 Finally, lay them flat on the compost (soil mix) surface, weighing them down so that they make full contact.

Planting slashed leaves

Use one large leaf from a rhizomatous begonia (e.g. *Begonia rex*), whose ovate, warty leaves can typically grow 20cm (8in) long, and sever it from the parent at the base of the stalk, which can then be discarded. Only use firm, healthy leaves. Then lay the leaf face down and make a number of 12mm (½in) long cuts, using a clean scalpel, across a dominant vein. Space out the cuts across the leaf so that the new plants are not all packed together.

Potting up

Lay the leaf, face up, on the top of the moist cuttings compost in a seed tray. Pin the leaf firmly down with the slashes in direct contact with the surface. New buds will develop at these points, producing plantlets and roots. Place the seed tray in a clear plastic bag to provide 21°C (70°F) warmth and humidity. After the plants appear in about four weeks, remove the tray and wait until they can be individually potted up.

Aftercare

Grow on the young plants in a shallow container until they are large enough to pot up individually.

RIGHT *Begonia masoniana*, distinguished by a dark brown-blackish mark like the German Iron Cross, can be propagated by leaf squares.

LEAF SLASHING FROM A BEGONIA

1 When slashing a begonia leaf, turn it face down and make sure that the quick, short cuts run across a strong, prominent vein.

2 Then turn the leaf face up and pin it on top of the compost (soil mix), ensuring that each slash is in contact with the surface.

ABOVE 'Etna' is a compact begonia with crimson-brown leaves that are splashed with bright patches of silver and pink.

ABOVE The puckered leaves of 'Helen Rowe' are an even creamy-green with ruffled, dark margins and a striking central mark.

ABOVE The cultivar 'Silver Jewel' needs good humidity at all times or it may shed its leaves, especially during cold periods over winter.

Root cuttings

There is nothing new about propagating from roots. It has been practised for well over 350 years, and though it has never become as popular as taking softwood cuttings, for example, it can be an incredibly successful way of making large numbers of new plants from a relatively small amount of material.

The simplest cut

A good way to show the power of roots to generate new plants is to dig quite fiercely in spring around a *Rubus*, for example, slicing the spade just under the surface. The aim is to sever through the roots. Remove the

ABOVE Phlox make a very impressive border show in cottage and formal gardens, but you will need several plants to create a strong impact. More plants can easily be propagated by taking root cuttings, by seed, softwood cuttings and division.

ABOVE The tender clerodendrums, mainly from near tropical regions, might die over winter so grow replacements as a precaution.

ABOVE The Chilean glory flower (*Eccremocarpus*) is usually grown from seed, but you can also opt for root cuttings.

ABOVE The subshrub *Romnya coulteri* is not reliably hardy; if you live in a chilly area, grow precautionary replacement root cuttings.

ABOVE In late summer *Campsis radicans* has orange-red flowers. Take precautionary replacement cuttings in cold regions.

parent plant, and make sure that the roots left in the ground are well watered in a dry spell. By autumn, they should have generated new growth that will be poking through the ground. Eventually, they can be dug up and replanted.

Timing

Different plants (and there are not that many that can be used for root cuttings) have different times when root cuttings are taken, but as a general rule stick to the end of autumn, and the start of the dormant period. Select a vigorous, well-established plant with a good root system, and carefully fork it out of the ground. If the plant is too large to get out, or the root system is proving immovable, you simply need to be able to get at the roots, in which case dig down until some are exposed.

The cut

With the plant out of the ground, wash or spray the root system to get rid of the mud and expose the growth. Then use a sharp, clean knife to slice off pencil-thick, fleshy lengths of root, taking each one

ABOVE The Indian bean tree (*Catalpa bignonioides*) makes a 10m (30ft) high specimen, and produces striking flowers.

from as close to the plant's crown as possible. Each length should be about 12.5cm (5in) long and at least 6mm (¼in) wide, with the cut closest to the crown and the soil surface being straight and the bottom one, further away in the soil, being angled. This will help you remember which is the top and bottom. The parent plant then goes straight back in the ground, at the same depth as before. Firm in well to ensure there are no air pockets, and water in well.

Potting up

These thick cuttings can then be inserted in pots – with say five to an 8cm (3½in) container – that have been filled with loam-based compost (soil mix) for standing in a cold frame. The pots must be deep enough to sink in the whole length

of root vertically, with the angled cut at the bottom, the straight cut just beneath the top covering of compost finished off with a scattering of grit. If the compost is already moist, do not water, but if it is dry just give a gentle drink. Expect to see results at the top within about 16 weeks, but if you need quicker results in a quarter of the time then take much shorter cuttings, 2.5cm (1in) long, and having potted them up provide mild bottom heat – about 18°C (65°F) – in a greenhouse.

Aftercare

If you have neither a cold frame nor a greenhouse, then cuttings of plants which are quick to produce new

roots – the tree of heaven (*Ailanthus altissima*) and *Rhus typhina*, for example – can be put in the open ground. When this new growth appears, you can start watering.

Horizontal cuttings

Plants with thinner, fibrous roots, such as *Campanula*, can be treated slightly differently. Do not bother making straight and angled cuts, because you do not need a top and bottom. Instead, the 7.5cm (3in) long cuttings are laid 2.5cm (1in) apart just below the compost on a seed tray, and are given a 12mm (½in) covering of grit on top of that. These cuttings might well generate growth at both ends.

TAKING ROOT CUTTINGS FROM A PHLOX

1 Sever the roots using a sharpened knife, making the cut close to the crown, that is topped by the surface growth.

2 To clearly mark a root's crown-end from the base, give the latter an angled cut and the former a straight cut.

3 Plant with the straight (top) cut just below the compost (soil mix) surface and cover with a layer of grit.

4 When using horizontal cuttings, lay them neatly in rows just below the surface, under a scattering of grit.

Plants that provide root cuttings

Campsis	Paulownia
Catalpa	Phlox
Clerodendrum	Romneya
Eccremocarpus	

Division

One of the quickest and easiest ways of propagating is digging up a plant that has become a packed clump of shoots or buds, and slicing it into smaller sections for replanting. Just double check that each division, or new plant, has the means to develop above ground with a few buds, and roots to anchor it in the ground and feed.

Propagating such clump-forming plants does two things. It provides new plants, and is an excellent way of preventing the parent plant (typically a herbaceous perennial) from gradually deteriorating in the centre, becoming a big disappointment, with all the best growth at the fringes. In the wild this does not matter, but who wants a feature border plant that is overcrowded and tangled and unproductive in the centre? Worse, the dying centre can become a breeding ground for pests and diseases. So, after several years of growth, before this happens, and before the plant starts producing fewer, smaller flowers, be brutal. Divide to produce fresh, new vigorous plants and start arranging them around the garden.

To cover all eventualities, the chapter tackles plants with fibrous roots, those with fleshy crowns, plants with suckers, those with rhizomes, plants producing offsets and runners, and ends with a special feature on dividing water lilies.

LEFT A newly divided batch of lilac irises. Give them space to multiply, which will guarantee a bright show and vigorous growth.

Dividing plants with fibrous roots

Herbaceous perennials with a tangled mass of thin, fibrous roots are relatively easy to divide, posing fewer problems than plants with a seemingly impenetrable, dense, thick, tough interconnecting root system. With luck, you can divide the former by hand; the latter inevitably involve a bit of muscle.

New from old

A young plant with fibrous roots has a rather loose crown with an abundance of buds in spring. As the plant gets older, so the crown becomes increasingly woody with fewer shoots. Division discards the old, relatively unproductive centre, and keeps the vigorous outer portions for replanting.

ABOVE Achilleas are mainly herbaceous perennials, and spread to make impressive clumps. But the moment they start to become tired and congested in the centre, dig them up, prise them apart and replant the more productive, younger, outer portions.

Digging up

The first job is to get the old plant out of the ground in early spring, when still dormant, just before it is about to break into new growth. This means that the new, young, replanted sections will quickly recover, while giving them one whole season to get established. Do the digging on a fine, mild day, when you and the plant are not battling with the elements. Carefully dig it up with a fork so that you do not damage the root system. This often sounds much easier than it is in practice, but persevere and it will come out. You might have to resort to a spade, getting it right under the plant before it will come out. Then snip off any dead top growth so that you can clearly distinguish between the old, deteriorating central portion and the newer, more vigorous fringe areas that you want to keep.

Separating

If you end up with a great big solid, muddy root ball (roots), and cannot see what you are doing, spray off some of the soil. If the soil is dry and loose, just shake it off. This helps you see where best to make the

ABOVE *Alchemilla mollis* makes an excellent filler in bare stretches at the front of the border, and tolerates long, dry periods.

ABOVE Essential ingredients in the late summer garden, asters need dividing every other spring to maintain a first-rate display.

Timing

The best time to undertake any activity is generally when you have the time and inclination to do a first-rate job. So if you cannot divide a summer-flowering plant in early spring or autumn, when dormant, or a spring-flowering plant in summer, after it has flowered – the ideal times when you have the best chances of getting a high success rate – then do it at another time, but always make sure that the replanted sections get a good regular drink in dry spells during the growing season.

ABOVE Bell flowers (*Campanula*) give a carefree cottage-garden look with a plethora of blues, as well as pink and white.

ABOVE Chrysanthemums generally need dividing every three years for a middle-of-the-border, colourful late summer show.

ABOVE Established geraniums can easily be divided, creating extra plants to fill gaps as they appear around the garden.

divisions. In the case of a large root system, spear one long fork into the clump, followed by a second, so that they are back to back, and then prise them apart. This might need quite a bit of force, rocking the two back and forth, until the clump splits apart. Each section can then be subdivided, giving several new plants. Check that each one has a few buds and a good root system. If either is missing, do not use it.

ABOVE Heleniums add colour through summer into early autumn, but they can become congested. Divide the clumps every three to four years, keeping the vigorous, outer sections.

ABOVE Hostas are best divided in spring before they have put on too much leafy growth, though late summer is possible.

Topping

If you are dividing a plant when the new sections have plenty of long, leafy top growth, immediately shorten this or the plant will quickly lose more moisture through the leaves than it can take up through the roots. Do not put it under stress at a time when it is still trying to get established.

Irishman's cuttings

Delphiniums and Michaelmas daisies (*Aster novi-belgii*) are good examples of plants that produce new stems, called 'Irishman's cuttings', right at the base, which already have their own root system. All you need do is carefully separate them from the parent, prising them away before planting them up.

ABOVE Fibrous-rooted evening primroses (*Oenothera*) can be divided in spring, adding rich yellow to the summer border.

ABOVE Monardas are very efficient spreaders, adding colourful verticals, and can be divided by severing the new growth.

ABOVE Penstemons are worth propagating because they are not all reliably hardy, and can easily die in heavy soil in a bad winter.

Alternative methods

If the clump is small, then just use a couple of hand forks or trowels. However, if you are really lucky, in the case of *Heuchera* and *Epimedium*, you can just pull the clump apart with your bare hands.

Aftercare

Look after the new plants, and give them the best possible start. If they are being planted in a part of the garden that does not have good, well-worked soil, dig a large hole, fork up the bottom to loosen the soil, plant so that the crown is at the same level as before, and then refill with a mix of the original soil and well-rotted organic material. Make sure that the plants are well firmed in, which will eliminate any air pockets. All this must be done immediately after separating so that the sections go straight back into the ground as soon as possible. Label the plants, water them in, keep the immediate area weed free, and remember to give them a drink

during dry spells. While they are getting established, these new young plants are still largely dependent on you.

Exceptions

If you are replanting in the same piece of ground as before, give the plants a kick-start with a slow-release

ABOVE For an attractive, continuous show of the bluish leaves of *Festuca glauca*, divide the plant every three years or so.

fertilizer. In the case of very small divisions, they may be better nurtured in a container in a cold frame (especially over the first winter) until they are larger and more robust, and are capable of surviving a particularly cold spell. Plant them out when they need less cosseting.

Dividing grasses

Cool-climate grasses (such as *Deschampsia*, *Festuca* and *Stipa*) that flower before midsummer are best divided in the autumn, late winter or early spring. Warm-climate grasses (*Miscanthus* and *Pennisetum*) that flower after midsummer need dividing (less frequently) in late spring. Dig them up, shorten the leaves to make it easier to work, then prise the clump apart by hand. If the roots will not yield, do not tug at them, inflicting extra damage, but slice through the clump with a knife or spade (and if that won't work, try a saw). Such divisions are an excellent way of creating more plants, for a row of grasses to fringe a path, for example.

ABOVE Black-eyed Susan (*Rudbeckia fulgida*) needs rejuvenating every five years or so to maintain its strong show of bright yellow.

ABOVE Speedwell (*Veronica*) can be easily propagated by dividing well-established plants in spring, or later, in autumn.

Fibrous-rooted plants for dividing every few years

Achillea	*Lythrum*
Alchemilla	*Monarda*
Alyssum	*Nepeta*
Armeria	*Oenothera*
Aster	*Ophiopogon*
Astilbe	*Penstemon*
Campanula	*Phlox*
Chrysanthemum	*Polemonium*
Delphinium	*Pyrethrum*
Dicentra	*Rudbeckia*
Erigeron	*Stachys*
Geranium	*byzantina*
Helenium	*Tiarella*
Hosta	*Trollius*
Ligularia	*Veronica*

DIVIDING AN ACHILLEA

1 Carefully fork the plant out of the ground, gradually working around and under it to free the roots on all sides.

2 Use a hand fork to scrape away the thick clumps of soil around the roots so that you can clearly see what needs to be done.

3 Thin the top growth, and remove any dead or dying stems, which can then be promptly discarded.

4 Insert two forks back-to-back, and then prise the clump apart. In tough cases you might need another person to help.

5 Separate the newer, more vigorous outer portions and replant them in well-weeded soil improved with well-rotted organic matter.

6 After firming in, water in well. Keep an eye on them during their first growing season and keep weeds well away.

Dividing plants with fleshy crowns

Plants with a sturdy, thick, compact crown and system of roots with an abundance of growth buds need special handling. When dug up and seen for the first time, you might think the best thing is to stick them straight back in the ground, and that they should not be touched, but these crowns are actually very easily and successfully divided.

Budding plants

The key point when dividing plants with such tough, dense crowns is identifying new sections with a number of growth buds, with the potential to provide vigorous new plants. These sections also need a

ABOVE Astilbes are a colourful mainstay of boggy sites, giving a showy display in colours ranging from white to red, pink and purple.

ABOVE Pretty blue delphiniums can easily be grown from seed, and you can raise all the extra plants you need by division.

decent root system, which both feeds and anchors the plant in the ground. One by itself is not enough.

Being brutal

In early spring, at the end of the dormant season, carefully dig up the plant and then try to get rid of as much soil as possible – hosing might help – so that you can clearly see what you are doing. The fleshy or woody crowns can be so tough that it is impossible to tear them apart by hand, and the only option is to use a sharp, clean knife or spade to slice straight through the crown and root ball (roots) where there is one or more natural divisions. If there are no obvious, natural divisions, then roughly divide the plant into several sections, and slice accordingly, trying

ABOVE The South African agapanthus can be highlighted in an ornamental pot, such as a Versailles planter, but the growth will eventually become so packed that you need to get the plant out or the show will start to deteriorate. Divide and replant in spring.

Plants with fleshy roots

Agapanthus	*Helleborus*
Anthropodium	*Hemerocallis*
Astilbe	*Hosta*
Delphinium	*Lupinus*
Dicentra	*Rheum*

to avoid damaging too many shoots. Do not limit a new section to just one latent shoot in case it does not develop, and you end up with a dud. Then check the roots, and trim any that have been damaged.

Stress management

Always replant the new sections as quickly as possible to avoid any drying out, and to keep stress to an absolute minimum. Larger sections should flower that season, but smaller ones will need another season.

Replanting

The new planting holes should be refilled with well-worked soil and well-rotted organic matter, with the crowns level with the ground and the shoots just above soil level. Do not replant them any deeper than before. Finally, water in well and keep the whole area well weeded. If you need to build up a large quantity of one particular plant, then divide the plant on a fairly regular basis. It is a fallacy that letting one plant build up into a large clump will instantly provide you with all the sections you need, in one go. It will not.

DIVIDING A HEMEROCALLIS

1 When digging up daylilies (*Hemerocallis*), spade the whole clump out of the ground, working around and under the root system.

2 Identify sections with growth buds on top and a batch of roots below, and then sever them away by slicing down with a spade.

3 Select good, solid new sections with their own root system clearly visible and the potential for top growth.

4 They can now be replanted in well-worked ground with some well-rotted organic matter. Weed carefully all around and water in well.

ABOVE The fragrant *Hemerocallis* 'Wind Song' adds a strong show of orange flowers, and contrasts well with rich blues and reds.

ABOVE Rheums are grown for their large leaves and towering flower spikes in bog gardens or areas with moist soil.

Slug patrol

When replanting in damp, shady conditions, do not forget that many plants (hostas being a prime example) are a magnet to slugs and snails. If pests promptly chomp through the new growth of young plants, they will, in time, seriously weaken them, and stop them becoming strong, vigorous specimens. No matter which solution you favour – beer traps, picking off by hand at night etc. – keep on top of the problem. If all else fails, grow the plants in raised containers, wrapping copper tape or strips around the outside to deter the slugs with a minor electric shock.

Dividing plants with suckers

Many shrubs naturally increase by sending out long underground shoots from the roots (as in *Rhus typhina*) or underground stems (*Gaultheria shallon*). They are a terrific source of new plants and are well worth propagating, not least because if left they might well overwhelm the parent.

Wait for the roots

If you spot what looks like one or more new young versions of the parent breaking out of the ground say 30cm (12in) or even further away, then carefully scrape back the soil at the start of spring and trace

their origin. You are looking for one underground stem per 'baby' leading straight back to the parent. If left, the new plants will gradually increase in size, eventually forming a thicket, with the new growth competing with the original plant for nutrients and water. If you do not want to propagate them, see the 'Suckers – bad news' box (below right).

Preparing suckers

Having exposed the join, look for a cluster of fibrous roots just below where the suckering stem emerges out of the ground. If they have not developed, firm back the soil and

ABOVE *Amelanchier lamarckii*, with white spring flowers, is best as an eyecatching small tree, without competing suckers.

DIVIDING A SUCKERING SHRUB

1 When the strong framework of a shrub is becoming fuzzy and cluttered with new suckering growth, it is time to act.

2 Scrape away at the soil around a sucker, and check to see that it has developed its own root system just under the soil.

3 Tug the sucker (its root system is obscured in this photo) away from the parent, and sever the length of stem beneath.

4 The new plant, with topgrowth and roots, can now be replanted elsewhere. Water in well and through the growing season.

Suckers – bad news

To get rid of unwanted suckers – and this could apply to trees as well as shrubs, especially if the tree's roots have been damaged in any way, perhaps by close mowing and striking the surface roots, or by close digging – take prompt action. If left unchecked, suckers could eventually turn into trees. Unearth the 'umbilical cord', tracing it back to the parent, then give a sharp tug to pull it away. This is better than a clean cut with secateurs, because the tugging pulls off any dormant buds that might grow at a later date, thus repeating the problem. Also note that suckers on roses (or any grafted plants) from the base will not reproduce the highly attractive top growth, but the rootstock plant, which is very different (the rootstock is like the plant's engine, providing the vigour but none of the glamour). You can immediately spot the sucker on a rose because it has different leaves and stems (in colour, size and shape). Also look out for suckers at the base of cultivars of witch hazel (*Hamamelis*) when it has been grafted on to *H. virginiana*. The leaves on the former will usually hang on for longer than the cultivar's.

ABOVE Lilacs (*Syringa*) give such a good display in late spring and early summer with their scented flowers that it is worth looking out for new suckering growths. When they have developed their own root systems they can be used as new plants.

ABOVE *Cornus sericea* 'Flaviramea' is grown for its yellowish-green winter shoots; it is also a prodigious suckering shrub.

wait for them to develop. The sucker will not survive without its own root system. Given they exist, sever the sucker from the parent with sharp secateurs, and then cut off the long length of sucker below the fibrous root system. This is completely redundant and you can immediately discard it.

Growing suckers

The young sucker can now be planted in the open in well-prepared ground, or nurtured in a container filled with potting compost (soil mix). Water it regularly in dry spells through the growing season. If the parent plant tends to be rather leggy, cut back the young plant to make sure that it becomes thick and bushy, or if the

root system looks too spindly at this stage to support a large amount of top growth. However, it is sometimes worth leaving suckers, for example on the stag's horn sumach (*Rhus typhina*), to create a clump with bonfire-coloured autumn leaves, before they fall.

RIGHT Bay (*Laurus nobilis*) is often grown in pots to avoid the winter wet, but in dry, mild areas it makes a large hedge.

Plants that sucker

Amelanchier	Rhus typhina
Cornus	Robinia
Forsythia	pseudoacacia
Kerria japonica	Salix
Laurus nobilis	Sarcococca
Populus	Syringa

ABOVE *Kerria japonica* makes a substantial shrub, a good 2m (6ft) high and 2.5m (8ft) wide, with a strong show of yellow spring flowers. Keep a constant lookout for its new suckering growth, and rip it away from the parent the moment it pokes through the soil.

Dividing plants with rhizomes

Many plants have thick root systems, often at soil level, resembling horizontal, solid, warped sausages – the branching rhizomes of root ginger being a good example. These rhizomes (often food stores) are actually modified stems, and can be divided to create new plants.

Perennials with rhizomes

The best garden examples are so-called bearded irises (though note that not all irises have rhizomes), and the best time to tackle them is straight after flowering in summer. That is when the new root system starts developing.

ABOVE Rhubarb (*Rheum*) provide plenty of leafy, impressive, subtropical growth in the damp soil around a natural pond or in a bog garden. They are also particularly impressive in summer when they are topped by an erupting mass of tiny, star-like flowers.

DIVIDING A RHIZOMATOUS IRIS

1 Carefully lift the packed clump, making sure that the prongs of the fork do not spear and damage the rhizomes.

2 Lay the sections on the soil, separating the new (with buds and foliage) for replanting; discard the old, unproductive parts.

3 Trim the foliage of the new, vigorous sections so that it will not catch the wind like a sail, and dislodge the rhizome in the soil.

4 Replant into crumbly, free-draining, well-worked, well-weeded soil. Keep watering over summer, while it is developing.

Separation, slicing and laying

Carefully dig up the plant with a fork, inserting the prongs into the ground away from the main clump to avoid spearing the rhizomes. Try to see exactly what you have got, either by shaking off the soil or, on a wet day, when it will not budge, by spraying it off with a hosepipe. Then pull the clump apart, separating the old, exhausted, unproductive rhizomes and those with dead flower stalks (which you will not need) from the new, young growth with buds and leaves (which you do need, for replanting). Handle with care.

Then comes the next stage. The new rhizomes can be sliced up into chunks about 7.5cm (3in) long using a clean, sharp knife (you can dust the cut surfaces with a fungicide to eliminate any possibility of infection and rot), but check that each piece has its own individual set of leaves and roots. The latter need trimming by about one-third if they are long; shorten the foliage to leave just 15cm (6in) of growth. This means that the plants will not lose more water than they can take up through their roots, and will not be blown about in strong winds, loosening the grip of their roots in the soil. Replant in improved soil.

Lay each rhizome horizontally in its own shallow hollow. It needs to be half-buried so that the back of each is visible (like a floating whale, part above and part below the water) with the leaves poking upwards, but the fibrous roots firmly set in the ground. Group them so that they are approximately 15cm (6in) apart.

Aftercare

Being exposed to the hot summer sun means they will dry out very quickly, and need to be regularly watered throughout the season. If you go away for a long, hot period, leaving no one in charge, you will come back to a cluster of dead, baked rhizomes. Do not be tempted to mulch them, covering them in a protective layer of soil, because this is counter-productive.

Crown rhizomes

Other typical rhizomatous plants include peonies and asparagus. Peonies pose a slightly tricky problem because

ABOVE The arum lily (*Zantedeschia*) brightens up areas of moist soil, producing flamboyant late spring and summer flowers.

they do not like being moved. They do best if the new divided clumps are quite big – small ones can take a long time to get established. They need digging up when the end of winter meets spring, when you can easily spot the new buds bulging out of the crown. Each new section must have a few buds (do not rely on just one in case it is not prolific), and again the cut surface can be dusted with fungicide. When replanting, keep the sections about 23cm (9in) apart.

ABOVE Cannas add a subtropical look to summer bedding schemes, with their large leaves and gladioli-like flowers.

Bamboos

These are best divided in mid-spring, but cut back the height of any tall canes or the plant will get rocked out of the ground in a high wind. Bamboos have comparatively shallow, anchoring roots. If you do not want to cut them back, ensure they are planted in a sheltered site to avoid wind problems. Failing that, tie them securely to a stout post, allowing for the fact that strong winds might strike from any direction.

ABOVE Asparagus have fleshy crowns prone to rotting, so avoid wet sites. If there is poor drainage, plant them on raised mounds.

ABOVE Mint (*Mentha*) is such a rampant spreader that it is usually grown in a deep bottomless bucket sunk in the ground.

ABOVE When replanting peony rhizomes, make sure that each has about four buds, and plant them about 2.5cm (1in) below the soil.

Dividing plants with offsets and runners

One of the key ways in which many plants multiply is by offsets and runners. The former is a young plant that is clearly joined to the parent, and which can be simply and quickly detached from it. The latter appears at the end of a long, horizontal stem that creeps across the soil, producing a rooting plantlet at the end.

Offsets

Clump-forming cacti and succulents, and many house plants – including pineapples (*Ananas*) – often produce new young plants at the base of the parent plant. They usually occur where there is a rosette of leaf growth at ground level (called basal leaves). Initially the expanding numbers of offsets can look incredibly impressive on the parent, creating a mounding, multiplying effect, but eventually they can overwhelm it, and you might run out of space.

Separation

To thin out and create extra plants, each of which in time will produce even more offsets, separate the

ABOVE After a mature agave has flowered, the rosette of leaves usually dies, being replaced by its offsets around the base.

ABOVE Many cacti, if given a regular summer feed and watering, produce a cluster of offsets around the base of the plant.

young plant – when it is clearly maturing – from the parent in spring. This can seem quite daunting, a bit like doing a miniature amputation. You should wear thick gloves when working on a spiky cactus. First, scrape back the compost (soil mix) to expose the join where the offset and parent meet. Then use a clean, sharp knife or scalpel, and carefully separate the two. Where the parent has been wounded, the exposed surface can be treated with a fungicidal powder.

Potting up offsets

The offset should be immediately potted up (one per small pot) in a free-draining compost, especially for cuttings. Just firm the base of the offset into the soil, and do not try planting it too deeply. Top the surface with extra grit and, while it is getting established, putting on anchoring root growth, keep it in light shade. This reduces the risk of dehydration, with more moisture being lost than can be taken up.

Runners

The best example of a runner is found on a strawberry plant (*Fragaria*). Neat, orderly rows of strawberries will quickly become a chaotic patchwork of plants if the runners are not kept in check. Strawberry plants usually last for three or four years before they start to decline, and these runners are an invaluable source of replacements.

Horizontal stems

Runners can be kept if you need to fill gaps in a new strawberry bed, or if you are expanding it. Otherwise they can be discarded until you need a new batch of plants to replace the

ABOVE Tender echeverias, often with yellowish-red flowers, can be planted out over summer to line the front of a border.

ABOVE Saxifrage quickly spreads and self-propagates thanks to its offsets, which can be easily removed and replanted elsewhere.

Plants producing offsets

Agave	Crassula
Cacti (e.g.	Echeveria
Echinocactus	Phormium
and	Primula
Mammillaria)	Sempervivum

ABOVE The blue-flowering *Ajuga reptans* spreads by stems that create new plants as they creep across the soil.

deteriorating, increasingly unproductive first batch of plants. Make sure that the parents are healthy, with flat, all-green leaves. Then, in early summer, select about four runners from each plant.

Potting up runners

Fill a pot with potting compost and set it in the bed, so that the compost is virtually flush with the surrounding ground. Then pin the horizontal stem in place in the pot, securing the plantlet. Make sure that it is watered during dry spells, and after about five weeks it should be ready for severing and planting out.

DIVIDING A SEMPERVIVUM

1 Look around the base of a sempervivum for offsets. Let them mature until they are getting bigger than a thumbnail.

2 With a long, sharp knife, slice one away from the parent making clean, sharp movements. Do not hack it off.

3 Carefully holding it by the edge of a leaf, lower it into cuttings compost (soil mix), firming it into a shallow hole.

4 Apply a scattering of gravel to the surface so that when giving it a drink the top layer of water quickly sluices away.

PEGGING A STRAWBERRY RUNNER

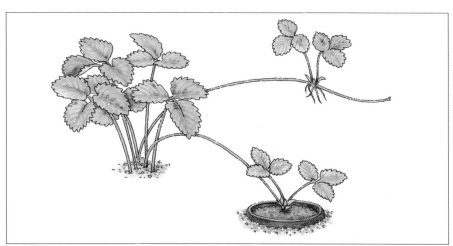

ABOVE Strawberry plants send out long stems (runners) across the soil. When they develop plantlets, insert a pot with cuttings compost (soil mix) in the soil below, and pin the runner in place with a U-shaped piece of wire. In five weeks it will be an independent plant.

Dividing water lilies

It is very tempting to think that you only need divide land plants that are gradually becoming congested, imagining that somehow water plants magically look after themselves. But some will need thinning, especially if they are grown in a small, submerged, aquatic basket. In larger ponds the divisions will make new plants. In both cases, the older, more unproductive sections are discarded.

Overcrowding

When a water lily (*Nymphaea*) becomes too congested every four years or so, its flowering potential significantly

ABOVE When buying a water lily, always check its eventual spread so that it does not choke your pond. Also keep an eye on its growth and performance. After about four years its rhizome might need slicing up, creating several more vigorous plants.

DIVIDING A WATER LILY

1 Hauling the plant out of its basket and out of the pond is the trickiest part. Once you have done that, clean the mud off the rhizome.

2 Either slice up the rhizome into sections, or, as here, remove a bud attached to a middle finger-length of rhizome.

3 Fill the container with aquatic compost and bury the bud, leaving the top exposed, then add a layer of shingle.

4 Then put this container inside a larger one, and fill the latter with water until it just covers the shingle. Keep in a cold frame.

diminishes. What you end up with is an abundance of leaves as the plant tries to absorb even more nutrients, from the water, to make up for the lack of them in the compost (soil mix).

Lifting

Lift the container out of the pond as spring turns to summer (avoid the very cold water before this time and the likelihood of new, young divisions rotting). There should be a new batch of leaves appearing. Carefully lift out the water lily, and then wash the soil off the roots, dipping them in the pond. You will be left with a thick, fleshy crown. The propagating technique is exactly the same as for any rhizomatous or tuberous plant with upward growth from a fleshy storage organ, with fibrous roots at the bottom. Use a knife to cut the organ into pieces; make sure that each one has buds for the top growth and a set of roots (trimming any that are too long).

Potting up

Insert the pieces in fresh aquatic compost, ensuring that there is a thin covering of soil topped by pea shingle, and then place the container inside a larger one filled with water to cover the shingle. The key point is that the top growth must be able to reach the water surface. If the water ledge is too deep, then stand the containers on a base to raise them up. As the plants mature, and the stems lengthen, so the containers can be submerged in deeper water.

Root buds

Some tuberous water lilies (and other rhizomatous and tuberous water plants) can instead be propagated by means of the small root buds emerging on the root stock. In spring break off a bud and plant it in aquatic compost in a small basket. If using a rhizomatous section, you need the bud still attached to about 8 cm (3½ in) of rhizome behind it. The bud should be semi-buried, with its growing tip left exposed. Top the surface with pea shingle, and then sit this basket in a slightly larger container. Fill it with enough water to just

ABOVE A water hyacinth (*Eichhornia*) produces the easiest kind of offsets; they can just be pulled off and lobbed back into the water.

cover the shingle, but no more, and keep it in the sheltered environment of a greenhouse. As the bud grows, so the depth of the water cover can be increased.

Plantlets

Some plants, such as water hyacinths (*Eichhornia*) and *Pistia*, produce small offsets that can be quickly pulled

ABOVE The floating aquatic *Pistia stratiotes* from the tropics and subtropics needs to be lifted and kept in the warmth over winter.

away from the parent. They do not need any special treatment, and can be put straight back in the water. Other plants – such as water soldiers (*Stratiotes aloides*) – produce their young like spider plants (*Chlorophytum*), with the parent sending out long stems and new young plants at the end. You can separate them when sufficiently large, with their own root system, placing them in shallow water.

Culling

Since water soldiers can become very large when mature, a good 75 cm (2½ ft) wide, they can quickly clog up a small pond or water channel with their widespread spiky leaves. In fact by late summer you will find a smallish pond is packed with layers and layers of plants, one on top of the other, making it impossible to see the bottom. A heavy cull is the only solution, keeping the new young specimens. Leave the discarded plants around the pond edge so that any wildlife (including newts) can waddle back into the water. Water soldiers are very good at keeping the water clear and oxygenated.

ABOVE Water lilies come in a wide range of colours from near blackish-red to bright whites. Their leaves help shade the water from the sun, reducing the amount of algae, and provide good hiding places for frogs which congregate beneath them.

Propagating Bulbs, Tubers and Corms

Many bulbs, tubers and corms naturally increase, and some eventually create an incredible spread or clump of colour. But not all are that quick to multiply, and it is often necessary to intervene and propagate, creating extra numbers.

At its simplest, this means detaching the new young miniature bulbs that appear beside the main bulb — and they will be exact copies of the parent, which cannot be guaranteed when taking seed. (Seed also takes far longer to produce a flowering plant.) Scaly bulbs can be tackled slightly differently, actually snapping off the scales that generate new young plants. Non-scaly bulbs can even be scooped and chipped, when they are either sliced up like an orange or have their bottoms scooped out like a hard-boiled egg. Tubers are usually easy to propagate, with shooting sections being separated and planted up. If you've got a handful of striking dahlias and want even more, this is a great way to generate fantastic blocks of colour.

This chapter covers everything you need to know, starting with removing offsets, bulblets and bulbils, before moving on to the best way to scale bulbs. It then explains scoring, scooping and chipping bulbs and, finally, ends with dividing tubers and corms.

LEFT A flamboyant show of *Narcissus* 'Pipe Major', which can be readily propagated, giving an extra show of yellow.

Removing offsets, bulblets and bulbils

Bulbs are highly efficient storage organs. They can survive long periods of dormancy below ground when the surface climate is hostile or unsuitable for growth. They are also capable of producing identical, miniature versions of themselves that provide quicker results than growing young plants from seed.

Terminology

There is occasionally some confusion as to the differences between these three terms. Here, to keep things simple, the young which are either attached to, or grow around the bulb, are called offsets. When they are attached below ground to the stem, they are bulblets, and when they appear above ground in the join between a leaf and the stem, they are bulbils. Crucially, all three can be detached and grown on before the bulb goes dormant, but note that different species have different dormant periods. Most are in active growth in spring and summer.

Why divide?

First, it can avoid an overcrowded, congested clump, with all the bulbs ending up – after many years –

ABOVE The bright orange, downward-pointing heads of *Fritillaria imperialis*. This exotic show is worth highlighting in a large tub.

packed together while competing for the same nutrients and moisture, resulting in poor performance. Second, you can create new groups of bulbs around the garden.

Offsets

The main characteristic of the offset is that it is usually found growing beneath the papery covering of the bulb (though not all bulbs actually have this), attached to the base, or possibly to the side or even beneath the bulb. Take great care when forking up a clump of, say, crocuses

ABOVE *Cardiocrinum giganteum* is a woodland bulb from the Far East; it likes rich, moist soil, avoiding hot, dry extremes.

or crinums, because it is very easy to spear them with the prongs. Then remove the soil to expose the offsets. The larger new ones can be planted out immediately, and should start

Plants producing offsets

Allium	*Gladiolus*
Cardiocrinum	*Leucojum*
Crinum	*Lilium*
Crocosmia	*Narcissus*
Crocus	*Scilla*
Fritillaria	*Tulipa*

REMOVING A TULIP OFFSET

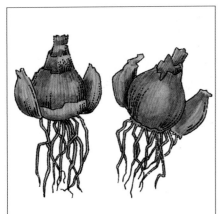

1 Dig up likely bulbs in spring, or after flowering, and look for mature offsets. If they are too small, leave them to grow.

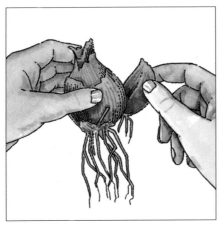

2 Detach the largest, by snapping them off crisply and cleanly. The bigger they are, the quicker they will be to flower.

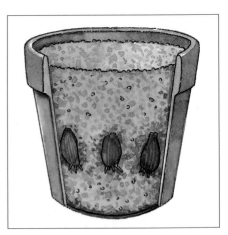

3 Plant them in a container at about twice their own depth, keeping them well apart so that they have plenty of room to fatten.

Lilies producing bulblets

Lilium auratum
L. longiflorum
L. speciosum

flowering the following year, with the smaller ones being nurtured in pots in a cold frame for up to two years. Plant them in groups, at twice their depth, in wide, shallow pots, making sure that each has room to double in size. The compost (soil mix) must be free draining. Water well in dry spells, but keep them much drier while dormant over winter. Otherwise, avoid any extremes that will put them under stress. The parent bulbs go straight back in the ground.

Bulblets

Not many plants produce bulblets, and rarely in big numbers, but do look for young, small bulbs on some lilies on part of the stem beneath the soil. The best time to remove them is at the end of summer. Set them out in a wide, shallow container, about 5cm (2in) apart with a covering of cuttings compost,

about one and a half times their own depth. After one year they should be ready for planting out, and will flower a few years after that.

Bulbils

Look for these tiny bulbs, which grow above ground on the stem, in the angle with a leaf. They should also be obvious, scattered on the ground where they fall, usually at the end of summer, and can be gathered up, taking care not to damage the tiny roots. Others can be removed direct from the stem. They need to be nurtured in a wide, shallow container, like bulblets.

REMOVING A LILY BULBLET

Lilies producing bulbils

Lilium bulbiferum
L. lancifolium
L. sargentiae

By removing the spent flowers of *L. candidum*, *L. x hollandicum*, and *L. x testaceum*, for example, bulbils will be generated.

Life and death

Some bulbs (e.g. *Cardiocrinum giganteum*) die after flowering, but automatically supply their own replacement offsets. They can be left where they are to flower.

1 After flowering, at the end of summer, look for small bulbs attached to the base of the stem, underneath the soil surface.

2 They can be easily plucked off between thumb and forefinger, and then lined up on a clean sheet of paper.

ABOVE Brighty coloured tulips need to be grown in decent-sized groups to provide maximum impact in the spring border.

3 Pot them up in a shallow container or small pots, setting them below the surface, at about one and a half times their own depth.

4 Scatter a thin covering of shingle on top, and then stand in a cold frame until they are large enough to be planted out in the garden.

Scaling bulbs

The technique of scaling is an extraordinary way of producing a large batch of new plants (especially lilies) from one scaly bulb, and is a good technique for getting children interested in something that they would normally run a mile from.

Clean snaps

Many bulbs (especially lilies) have a quite distinct covering of scales, and well over half, but no more than 75 per cent of those on one particular bulb, can be used to propagate new plants. Do this at the end of summer for plants due to flower next spring/summer, and in spring for the autumn/winter flowering kind. Also make absolutely sure that the parent is a solid, healthy bulb without any defects. Then bend back and snap off the fresh, healthy scales (discarding the discoloured, disfigured outer ones), making sure that each has a piece of the base. Strangely, the parent bulb does not suffer and it will flower as normal, on time, the following year. Its performance is not diminished by the scaling.

ABOVE After propagating bulbs, it is important to remember where you have planted the new sections in the garden. Use large stones that will not get kicked out of the way to mark their position, and then you will not risk digging them up and losing a lily display as good as this.

Storing

To safeguard the scales, and eliminate any chance of rotting, they need to be placed in a clear polythene or plastic bag and dusted with fungicide. Give a good shake to ensure that all parts are treated. Then pour in an equal parts mix of vermiculite and peat (or a substitute), so that the bag is just over half full, but no more. If you are propagating a lot of scales from several large bulbs, do not try cramming them all into the one bag; you need to make sure that there is approximately four times the volume of the vermiculite-and-peat mix to the volume of scales. A rough check will suffice. Then blow into the bag until it is fully inflated (but not to bursting point) and tightly seal it. Then keep it in a warm, dry, dark place at 21°C (70°F). If placed in direct sun the internal temperature will soar.

New growth

In approximately eight to twelve weeks, small bulblets (initially tiny white growths that produce roots and leaves) will appear on the scale's base. The bulblets-cum-attached-scales are now planted in free-draining potting compost (soil mix). It does not matter if part of the scale is poking above the compost surface, provided the bulblet is just under the surface, at twice its own

ABOVE *Fritillaria michailovskyi*, a stocky species from Turkey, reintroduced in 1965, has early summer brownish-purple flowers.

ABOVE Buying large numbers of new lilies can be expensive, which is why it makes good sense to propagate from your own stock.

SCALING A LILY BULB

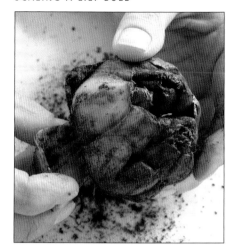

1 When the lilies' leaves have died down in late summer, or soon after, select a firm, healthy bulb and start pulling off the scales.

2 You should now be left with several scales, and provided you do not massacre the parent, it will continue to flower well.

3 When putting the scales in a plastic bag, they need to be treated with fungicide (in liquid or powder form) to prevent rotting.

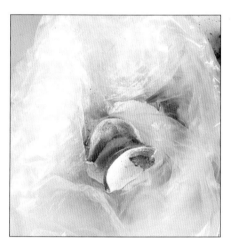

4 Give the bag a gentle shake so that all sides of the scales are covered with the fungicide. To avoid any damage, don't be too vigorous.

5 Half-fill the bag with a 50:50 mix of perlite or vermiculite and peat (or a substitute). Or just use perlite, as shown here.

6 Finally, blow into the bag to inflate it and tightly seal, and keep in the warmth until small bulblets start to appear.

depth. Finally, top the surface with grit, and stand the pots outside for summer in a cold frame in the shade.

Potting up

The attached piece of scale soon dies, leaving the bulblets, and they can be gently removed for replanting in pots at regular, wider spacings in autumn when the leaves have faded. Then stand the pots in a cold frame over winter. The following spring and summer they can be potted up as necessary, as they grow, being planted out when they reach flowering

size. Or plant out after their third year, but it could take two more years before they flower. Keep an eye out for lily beetles. An infestation of these 8mm (⅓in) long bright red beetles with a black head can ruin the top growth. Pick them off when seen, as with slugs, putting a sheet of newspaper on the ground under the plants to catch any beetles that fall. Immediately crush them.

RIGHT *Nomocharis* is related to the lily, and has scaly bulbs that can be used to create extra clumps of early summer flowers.

Scoring, scooping and chipping bulbs

These techniques might sound like something out of a cookbook, but all three are extremely easy, and are best used on plants that are slow to produce their offsets. They speed things up quite quickly.

Scoring

Simply turn the bulb (for example a fritillary) upside down in late summer, and make two or three slicing cuts, as if you were going to divide the bulb into sections. But the knife should not cut any deeper than 6mm (¼in). The cuts then

ABOVE Snowdrops (*Galanthus*) can be propagated by scoring or scooping, and thrive in sites with plenty of winter and spring rain with hot, dryish summers, though they do not like being baked. Most species flower in late winter or early spring.

SCORING A HYACINTH BULB

ABOVE An upturned hyacinth bulb clearly showing the four shallow cuts on the base plate where the new bulblets will appear.

SCOOPING A HYACINTH BULB

need to be dabbed with sulphur dust to counter any infection. Finally, spread a thick layer of moist sand in a saucer, just enough to sit the upside-down bulb on, keeping it upright. It then goes into an airing cupboard (or a warm, dry, dark place) for about 12 weeks, when the bulblets will appear. They, and the attached bulb, now need to be planted (still upside down) in a small pot. The compost (soil mix) should just cover the small bulblets. At this point they can go into a greenhouse, being placed in a cold frame in spring. After 12 months the bulblets can be

separated, and given their individual pots. Plant out when they have reached flowering size. This method produces fewer, larger bulblets than scooping, which is the second option.

Scooping

Slightly trickier than scoring. You need an old teaspoon with one sharp edge. Then take a hyacinth bulb, for example, in later summer and scoop out the inner portion of the basal plate, as if you were scooping the top out of a boiled egg. Leave the outer rim of the plate, and the exposed base of the bottom scales.

1 Hold a large, healthy bulb upside down and use a teaspoon, ideally with a sharp edge, to scoop out the inside of the base plate.

2 Do not damage the shell or casing of the bulb, but do expose the bottom of the scales. This is then dusted with fungicide.

3 After it has been stood bottom-up in moist sand in the dark, new growth eventually appears, providing firm, young bulbs.

CHIPPING A NARCISSUS BULB

1 Begin by trimming the roots, getting rid of any wispy lengths, but do not damage the base plate. Then slice off the nose.

2 Now cut down into the bulb, slicing it up into equal segments. The key point is that each must have part of the base plate.

3 Each segment must be treated with a fungicide, then insert into a plastic bag with vermiculite. Inflate, seal and keep warm.

That is crucial. The whole of the base is then dusted with fungicide to avoid rot, after which the process is very similar to scoring. The bulb is set bottom-up on a bed of moist sand in a saucer, and kept in the dark and warmth. When a batch of bulblets appears on the cuts, after about 10 weeks, the bulb is put in a pot filled with compost. The bulblets should be just below the surface. Keep the pots in a cold frame until spring. Gradually the parent bulb disintegrates, and the young bulbs can be separated and given small, individual pots. Keep nurturing until they have reached flowering size after three to four years.

Chipping

Sometimes called sectioning, this does actually involve slicing up the non-scaly parent bulb, for example a hippeastrum, which is particularly tricky to propagate. It also has a higher success rate than scaling. Start with a firm, healthy, dormant bulb – and note that good hygiene is very important to avoid the likelihood of infection with this technique. Clean it by stripping off the papery covering (if present), and then trim

off the roots using a sterilized knife, but do not cut into the basal plate. The bulb's nose also needs slicing off. Then divide the bulbs like an orange, slicing it into segments (approximately 12), checking that each has a piece of the basal plate. The segments then need to be treated with sulphur dust in a clear plastic bag or, to be ultra careful, soak them in liquid fungicide and then drain. Finally, moist vermiculite

is added and the bag is blown up, as with scaling, and sealed, being kept in a warm, dark place. Within about three months bulblets will have formed. The segments can then be potted up, so that the bulblets have a covering of 12mm (½ in) of compost. As the bulblets grow and develop roots, so the attached segments disintegrate, and each bulblet can eventually be given its own individual pot.

ABOVE Chipping is an excellent way of propagating an amaryllis (*Hippeastrum*), which cannot be grown from seed.

ABOVE Richly scented hyacinths need to be given a sunny sheltered site so that their wonderful scent can linger in the air.

Dividing tubers and corms

Like bulbs, tubers are underground storage organs, albeit structurally different, being swollen roots (just think of a potato) or stems, while the distinguishing feature of a corm (a swollen stem) is that the old corm withers and dies each year and is replaced by a new one. Both tubers and corms can be easily propagated.

Tubers

A dahlia is a typical tuberous plant. Dig it up after just one season and there will be a cluster of tightly packed underground organs, and after a few years of multiplying growth the cluster can become enormous.

If you need to dig dahlias up for overwintering in a cool, dry place before potting up next spring, these large clusters can become a nuisance. It is far better to divide them up, which also generates new individual plants. Each division must have a

ABOVE Tuberous dahlias come in a huge range of colours from the bright and brash to the subtlest pastels, and give a long show through the second half of summer to the end of autumn, when the leaves are blackened by the first frosts.

growth bud or eye, but if they are tricky to spot, lay the clump half-buried in a tray of compost (soil mix) in late winter, provide gentle bottom heat and spray with water. When the shoots develop on a particular tuber, separate it (complete, with roots at the bottom), and plant in a pot, with the new shoot just below soil level. Any cut surfaces need treating with a fungicide, followed by a drying out period when the surface heals.

You can alternatively cut off the young shoot, when 7.5cm (3in) long, then trim it just below a node, and treat that as a cutting, again potting it up in its own container. Keep both the potted tubers and cuttings well watered in dry summer spells, only planting them out when they are mature and well established.

Corms

Readily identified because they are shorter, wider and more solid than bulbs, the most crucial fact when it comes to propagation is that the new internal growth emerges from the centre. So, when slicing up a large corm just before it needs planting

ABOVE South African gladioli need a warm site and free-draining soil to thrive; heavy, cold, wet winter soil will rot the corms.

ABOVE Just a handful of freesia corms make a fine indoor pot plant display for spring. Pot up at intervals to give an extended show.

out, divide it into orange-like segments with each one having a bit of the central growing point, otherwise it will be a dud. The cut surfaces need be dusted with sulphur powder, and after drying and healing for 48 hours they can be planted up individually with the tops just protruding above the soil level.

Cormels

Freesias and gladioli readily produce large numbers of cormels (or offsets) between the old and the new corm. The shallower the parent is planted, the more offspring it should eventually produce.

When lifting the corms before their dormant period, remove the cormels and keep dry and frost-free in a plastic bag with air holes, filled with moist vermiculite, until ready for planting out next spring. Do not expect an immediate show of flowers. That might take approximately two years.

ABOVE Choose wisely and you can have crocuses in flower from autumn to spring. Some are gently scented.

DIVIDING A DAHLIA

1 Lift the tubers from the ground. Carefully insert the fork under and around them, taking great care not to spear and damage them.

2 Once you have dug up the tubers, gently clean the excess soil from them. Ensure that you label them for later identification.

3 Divide the tubers in late winter. Before making a cut, check that each tuber has an eye that will produce the top growth.

4 In this close-up view, the eye can be seen just to the left of the knife blade. New shoots will eventually be produced from the eyes.

5 Fill trays 10cm (4in) deep with moist, soilless compost and plunge the tubers shallowly into the surface, remembering to label the trays.

6 Water the compost when it starts drying out, and new shoots should appear quite soon. Ideally, provide bottom heat in a propagator.

Layering

The method of layering is one of the simplest kinds of propagation. Nature occasionally does it for you. When a strawberry plant sends out a runner, you sometimes find that the end, with a batch of fresh, young leaves, has rooted in the soil, producing a new plantlet. All you have to do is sever the 'umbilical cord', carefully prise the roots of the new plant out of the ground and find the best possible site for it. Since this is not that common, layering involves ingenious ways of tricking plants into doing something similar. The good news is that all of the action takes place outdoors.

There are seven basic layering methods described in this chapter. The first two involve simple and serpentine layering, in which stems are bent down to the soil, where they eventually take root and become independent plants. The third involves tip layering, in which just the tip produces a new young plant. The fourth involves stooling, when a plant is cut back to generate new replacement growth, with all the new shoots becoming new plants. The fifth is French layering, in which plants are again cut back but the new growth is stretched out around the parent to produce new plants. The sixth, dropping, involves 'dropping' a plant into a deeper hole to generate new plants. Finally, there is air layering, a rather tricky technique involving stiff, upright stems.

LEFT Grow a wisteria from seed and it may take a good 18 years before it is large enough to flower, but if you layer a new wisteria, not only will it flower within two or three years, but the colour will be exactly the same as the parent plant.

Simple and serpentine layering

A reliable means of propagating which anyone can master, layering takes very little time to set up but does then require a fair bit of patience (about a year) as you let the new plant take root. If you want more camellias, daphnes and jasmine, try it. Simple and serpentine layering both involve using long, bendy lengths of growth that have been wounded, to generate more plants.

Simple layering

This propagation technique could not be easier. If possible, select your parent plant one season before you aim to layer, and prune it back to generate lots of new, vigorous, bendy growth. This flexibility is essential because selected stems have got to be bent right down to the soil without snapping or breaking. Any plant producing long, supple stems can be layered in this way.

The time to act is when the plant is dormant between autumn and the approach of spring. It is probably best to layer one or two extra stems

ABOVE The smoke bush (*Cotinus coggygria*) has richly coloured leaves that turn orange in autumn. It is suitable for simple layering.

just in case the first one does not take successfully, so you do not have to waste time repeating the whole operation.

Selecting the right shoot

Use new, long, straight growth – not too thin and without any side shoots. Bend it gently down to the ground and select a leaf node that is about 30–45cm (12–18in) from

the growing tip, and that easily comes into contact with the soil. You do not want to force it.

Weeding

Now you know where the new plant is going to grow, you have got to prepare the ground. Weed a wide circular patch, say 15cm (6in) radius, to make sure there is no competition for water and nutrients, and so that you can clearly see how the new plant is developing.

The patch also needs to be dug over. If the ground had to be improved for the parent plant, make sure the space for the new plant is similarly treated. If it was heavy clay, add some well-rotted compost and grit to break it up and improve the soil structure and drainage. The crumblier it is, the better. If it was too poor and free-draining, again add some compost. You can, alternatively, put a container with potting compost (soil mix) in the ground and root the stem in that. The side of the hole nearest the plant should slope toward it, while the farthest side should be vertical.

Preparing the stem

The part of the stem that is in contact with the soil needs to be damaged or constricted to encourage the growth of roots. The easiest way to do this is by wounding the stem, giving it a little nick or cut on the

ABOVE *Actinidia kolomikta* is suitable for propagation by layering. It has white and pink new leaves, and white summer flowers, and needs a sunny, sheltered site.

ABOVE The long, bendy growths on a camellia give good results when layered. The new plants need acid soil and a sheltered site to avoid cold winds and damaging frosts.

underside with a sharp knife, just below (i.e. behind) a node. Gently prise back a bit of bark, and then add a dab of hormone rooting powder. Strip off any leaves that might be in contact with the soil.

Then create a 15cm (6in) hole, and gently bend the stem down into it. Pin the wounded piece in place with U-shaped galvanized wire, and fill the hole, covering the wounded section, gently firming the soil down to exclude any air pockets. Give it a drink. The end of the stem, approximately 15cm (6in) long, needs to be tied to a vertical cane.

Clearly mark the area, encircling it with canes and rope to keep people well away so that no one damages the growing tip. If you spot any subsequent weeds emerging through the soil, quickly remove, roots and all.

ABOVE For extra numbers of the Japanese snowball bush (*Viburnum plicatum*), propagate by layering the stems when dormant. Established plants reach 3 x 4m (10 x 12ft).

LAYERING A SHRUB

1 Lay down the stem, identifying where you want the new roots to grow, and the position in the soil for the planting hole.

2 The area for and around the hole needs to be well weeded and, if necessary, add some well-rotted organic matter.

3 Gently nick the stem, where the new roots are to grow, just behind a node. Use a clean sharp knife.

4 Then lift the bark and add a dab of rooting powder beneath it. The easiest way to do this is by using a paintbrush.

5 Make a small hole and pin the wounded section in place and bury it. Ideally, it should be 15cm (6in) deep, but can be shallower.

6 Finally, insert a vertical cane in the ground next to the end of the stem, so that you can tie it in, encouraging upright growth.

ABOVE The long, young, supple, flexible stems of a honeysuckle (*Lonicera*) are suitable for simple and serpentine layering, thus creating extra plants for a row of richly scented climbers. They are ideal for growing into small trees and for training over walls and fences.

ABOVE Clematis can be easily propagated by serpentine layering, which involves multiple woundings in a long stem.

Aftercare

Make sure the patch of ground stays weed-free, and water well in dry spells. It will take 12–24 months for a layered plant to root well. Different plants root at different rates, so be patient. Gently expose the soil beneath to see if it has rooted, and then give it several more months to develop and start growing vigorously. Sever it from the parent, lift and transplant in autumn or spring, being careful not to damage the new roots. It is important that its new growing position is weeded and, to help the plant through prolonged dry periods, add a mulch after the soil has been well watered.

ABOVE The best daphnes have such a ravishing scent that it is worth layering more to feature around the garden.

ABOVE Propagate *Pittosporum* shrubs because they are not reliably hardy, and you might need a replacement after a bad winter.

ABOVE Rhododendrons are an obvious choice for acid soil, and extra numbers can be propagated by simple layering.

ABOVE The climbing grape vines (*Vitis*) are grown for their reddish-yellow autumn leaves and stems, which are easily layered.

Serpentine layering

If you need more than one new plant, or are worried that one alone might not take, serpentine is a basic extension of simple layering. If you can do that, you can do this. It is an excellent technique for plants such as clematis, honeysuckle, rambling roses and wisteria.

Instead of making one wound in the stem, which is then buried in one shallow hole to take root, you use one long length of stem and wound it at regular intervals. Each wounded part creates a new plant in its own

ABOVE The magnificent flowering display of a wisteria can be grown against a wall, over a pergola or even through a sturdy tree, using it as a prop. The Chinese types flower in late spring, and the Japanese several weeks later. Propagate it by serpentine layering.

hole. So, for example, there might be three holes in a row, with the stem snaking in and out of each.

Make sure that the wounds are inflicted between the nodes this time, so that they are clearly visible on the length of stem (which has been stripped of its leaves) between the buried sections.

If these exposed nodes start generating new growth, which will obviously be clearly visible, nip it back so that the plants' energy is channelled into making plenty of root growth instead.

Self-layering

Some plants do the job for you, with ivies often rooting along the ground as they spread. Sever the new plants from each other and the parent, and then transplant or pot up. Keep giving regular drinks, and move into a larger pot when the roots poke out of the bottom.

Plants for serpentine layering

Campsis	Lonicera
radicans	Vitis
Clematis	Wisteria

As with simple layering, make sure each buried section has a patch of weed-free ground and is watered in; water again in dry periods. The holes should be 10cm (4in) deep, with both sides being gently slanted. You only need a far vertical side with a cane on the very last hole.

Tip layering

Blackberries and loganberries naturally propagate themselves when a stem flops on to or trails along the ground, and the tip roots where it comes in direct contact with the soil. This technique simply copies nature, and takes advantage of the fact that such plants have a strong concentration of rooting hormones right at the end of the stem.

Single tip layers

The easiest kind of tip layering simply involves taking one or several long, strong, new arching stems in summer, and bending them down to the ground. Where the tips meet the soil, either dig a hole for each approximately 10cm (4in) deep or fix a container with potting compost (soil mix) in the ground. In both cases make sure the surrounding area is weed-free. If digging a hole, make sure that the side nearest the parent plant is sloping toward it, that the far side is vertical, and that it can be refilled with fine, crumbly, free-draining soil, adding grit if necessary and well-rotted organic matter to improve the structure.

ABOVE Blackberries can be grown in two ways, neatly tying them up or, as here, letting them form massive, coiling mounds which double as an impenetrable hedge at the perimeter of a wild garden where it is a fight between gardener and birds for the crop.

Locking in place

Each tip then needs to be put head-down in the hole, being held in place by a strong piece of U-shaped wire. You can make the stem leading to the hole doubly secure by tying it to a stout cane fixed vertically in the ground by the hole or container.

Water the tip layer, and make sure you give it a regular drink during dry weather. When a new shoot appears above ground approximately three weeks later, check that it has rooted. Now cut the linking stem to the parent, but leave the new, young plant where it is growing until next

TIP LAYERING A BLACKBERRY

1 Bury the tip of the blackberry in a shallow hole, pinning it in place with a bent piece of wire. Water as required.

2 When the buried tip has developed its own root system and new top growth, it can be severed by the pin, but let it develop *in situ*.

spring. Then dig it up and plant; make sure that it is well tended throughout its first year.

Multiple tips

If you want a large batch of new plants, it is worth trying the following. Instead of using one long, new stem, select a short stem, about 40cm (16in) long, that has grown this current year. Then nip it back to force out new replacement growth. These new stems can in turn be nipped back, generating yet more new growth. And each one of these tips will now, come midsummer, be used to produce a new plant.

ABOVE *Rubus thibetanus* makes a thicket of white stems, a striking sight that looks best in full sun in winter.

Pinning in place

Though there are several shoots, you need just one hole, or possibly a short trench, in which to bury the tips. Again make sure the tips are pinned in place, and that there is plenty of fine soil for burying the tips, and keep the young plants well watered in dry spells.

ABOVE The ornamental *Rubus odoratus* grows 3m (10ft) high and wide, and produces pink flowers right through summer.

Colonization

Blackberries need regular care. They can form impenetrable, spiky mounds with powerful stems that can easily reach 4m (12ft) long. Train them along horizontal wires attached to posts, and cut out the old stems after they have fruited, to make caring (and picking) easier.

ABOVE If you want a cross between a raspberry and a blackberry, try a loganberry.

ABOVE Blackberries can be grown along a system of strong horizontal wires to make the picking process much easier. If left untouched, they will create a large, tangled, self-supporting mound.

Stooling and French layering

Also known as mound layering, stooling is an easy way of generating a large number of new plants from one shrub, and is particularly useful when you need a big batch of young plants to grow a uniform hedge. French layering is equally good at producing multiple new plants from one parent.

Stooling

The technique of stooling is most widely practised by commercial growers to produce virus-free rootstocks for fruit trees, guaranteeing their size and vigour. However, it can certainly be used at home on a few woody plants (for example dogwoods, lilacs and willows) that respond well to an annual cut, and is extremely productive. The most important point is that they are growing on their own roots, and have not been grafted on to another rootstock. If that has happened, you will be reproducing the plant with that particular root (used for vigour, not looks) and not the top, grafted part of the plant.

ABOVE The common lilac (*Syringa vulgaris*) can be stooled for a showy touch in late spring and early summer, before the garden's main display. It is a useful addition in an informal wildlife hedge, where it will attract privet hawk-moths, chaffinches and goldfinches.

The first cut

When using a new plant, let it establish for one season before cutting back the stems the following early spring. This cut needs to be approximately 3.5cm (1½in) above ground. The plant will quickly respond in the only way it knows how, by generating new replacement growth, and once this is 15cm (6in) long you need to act fast and cover 99 per cent of it with a well-prepared mound of soil, blocking out the light. The soil should have been well worked, being fine and crumbly. Avoid using large, solid lumps of

ABOVE Stool *Amelanchier laevis* to make a small tree or large shrub which, in late spring, is thickly covered in white flowers.

ABOVE The shrubby hazel *Corylus avellana* can be stooled to create new plants which have a good winter show of catkins.

ABOVE Rootstocks, grown to produce productive fruit trees at a certain height, are often propagated by stooling.

ABOVE The grow-anywhere Japanese quince (*Chaenomeles*) stands out in spring, with its bright flowers on the stiff, leafless stems.

ABOVE Willows (*Salix*) can be cut back hard for stooling, creating new shoots which gradually become independent new plants.

ABOVE Crab apples (*Malus*), grown for their clusters of brightly coloured ornamental fruit, can be increased by stooling,

clay, which need to be broken up with grit and well-rotted organic matter. Just leave the tips showing, making sure that the soil is firmed down between the emerging growth.

Repeat mounding

As the new growth lengthens, so it will need to be covered probably twice more, with the last mounding happening just after midsummer. Make sure you keep the immediate area weed-free to avoid competition for moisture and nutrients, and always water during dry spells to generate good new growth. Avoid the temptation to keep scraping back the soil to see what is happening beneath because you might well end up damaging the new growth.

Tree coppicing

Stooling and coppicing are often used as interchangeable terms, but that is when they refer to cutting a tree back to near its base. The technique forces the tree to generate new shoots, and this burst of thin growth is then used to make fences or poles. (When a tree is coppiced at head height, that is known as pollarding.)

Winter harvest

When the plant is dormant and the leaves have fallen, gently scrape back all the mounded soil to expose the buried, lower stems that will by now have developed clusters of roots at the base. Using a pair of secateurs, the rooted stems are severed from the parent plant, but make sure that when cutting them away the cut is flush to the stool. Also take care not to damage the roots. Each new rooted section can now be planted in its final position.

STOOLING A HEATHER

1 Make sure that the soil has an added mix of sand and compost or peat, and mound it around and between the stems.

More stools

That is not the end of the story, because the parent can be used to keep producing more plants by the same method. Clean the soil away from the remaining, exposed stub, and make sure that the surrounding soil has been weeded and given an all-purpose feed. If the parent and soil are well cared for, you will get many years of new plants. Plants that can be propagated in this way include *Amelanchier*, dogwoods (*Cornus*), lilacs (*Syringa*) and willows (*Salix*).

2 Leave just the last 3.5cm (1½ in) of each tip showing, and keep mounding up as the stems grow. Keep watering in dry spells.

French layering

Similar to stooling, French layering is popular with commercial growers who need a regular supply of a particular rootstock. It is also like serpentine layering, except the latter can be used on plants with supple, bendy growth that can be made to snake up and down into the soil, while French layering is used on plants with stiff, inflexible growth.

The technique is best used by amateurs when they need large numbers of a plant to create an impressive block of colour.

First steps

Using a young, established plant, cut it hard back in spring leaving about 3.5cm (1½in) of growth above ground. This in time will generate a handful of new shoots that will produce the new plants. At the same time, cut back hard any shoots that you do not need. Toward the end of winter stretch out this new growth along the ground, radiating it out from the parent plant. Pin it in position, and wait for new shoots to emerge from along the length of each stem. When the shoots are the length of a little finger, the long, laid-out stems can be carefully released, and the surrounding soil now needs to be well prepared; break it up, hitting any large clumps with the back of a fork, and add plenty of well-rotted organic matter. Make sure all weeds are promptly removed.

Trenching and covering

Dig long, narrow, 5cm (2in) deep trenches where the stem lengths were lying. Each stem can now be laid in

ABOVE The vigorous, deciduous *Hydrangea paniculata* produces a big burst of late summer, early autumn flowers.

its own trench and buried, leaving just the tips of the new shoots showing. As the shoots grow, keep mounding up soil around them, so that light is excluded from the base of each. Alternatively, leave the stems pinned to the ground and mound the soil over them, dispensing with the need for digging a trench. In early winter, when the mounds are about 15cm (6in) high, it is time to gently scrape back the soil to expose the join between the shoot and the laid out length of stem.

ABOVE An essential feature in the winter garden, dogwood (*Cornus*) has a thicket of bare, brightly coloured stems that will be beautifully highlighted in full sun.

Plants for French layering

Not many plants are propagated in this way, but they include:
Cornus
Cotinus coggygria
Hydrangea paniculata
Prunus tenella
Pyrus
Salix
Viburnum

And rootstocks of:
Malus
Prunus (cherry and peach)

Separating new plants

With all the underground growth now completely visible, the join between the underground stem and the parent is severed with secateurs. Then each new plant (the vertical growth and the roots at the base) can be severed from its neighbours for replanting. If you are going to need even more plants, the new, vigorous growth from the centre of the parent will become the next batch of stems for laying out. Once you have set out the new young plants in their final positions, keep watering thoroughly in dry spells so that the roots are not tempted to stay near the surface.

ABOVE The smoke bush (*Cotinus*) has the twin benefits of bright autumn leaf colours and a mass of tiny flowers, giving a blurring effect.

ABOVE *Prunus tenella* is one of the smallest cherries, just 1.5m (5ft) high and wide. The pink flowers are followed by velvety fruit.

FRENCH LAYERING A CORNUS

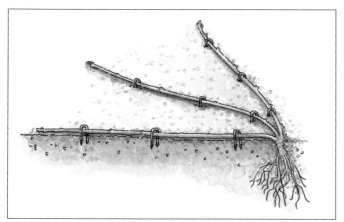

1 Cut back the top growth hard, just above soil level, to generate a batch of vigorous new shoots which are pinned to the ground.

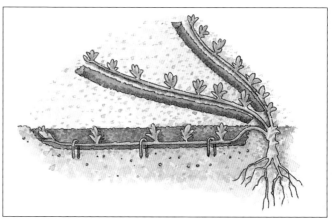

2 When new shoots have started emerging, dig a trench for the stems and keep mounding soil up above the new growing tips.

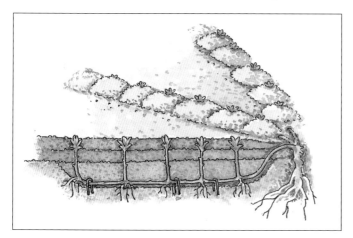

3 Keep repeating the mounding process. You can instead make individual soil mounds around the new growth and dispense with the trench.

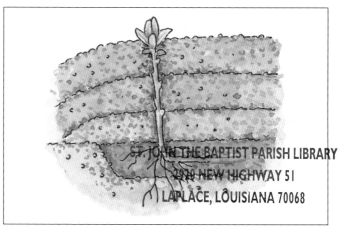

4 Eventually, you will have a series of new plants, each with its own set of roots. Sever these plants from the parent for replanting.

Dropping

Rarely practised by amateurs, dropping is well worth knowing about. It is ideal for a range of short, woody plants that do not produce long flexible stems for bending down to the ground for propagating by layering. Instead, you bury a plant, remove the new, young rooted growth, and then completely discard the parent.

Why drop?

When a short, shrubby plant is clearly past its best, with a rather desolate, open, unproductive centre, and straggly growth to the sides, do not abandon it. Instead, use it to generate a batch of vigorous young

ABOVE *Erica carnea* at its late winter best, with a great spread of purple flowers. It will tolerate mildly alkaline soil.

ABOVE *Erica vagans* 'Valerie Proudley' has a bright mix of yellow leaves and white flowers from midsummer through autumn.

replacements. Start by giving the plant a hard, all-over prune in winter, while dormant, to force out plenty of replacement growth the following spring that will root far more readily than the old, unpruned growth. Alternatively, you could buy one young, productive, bushy plant specifically for the purpose of dropping, and use that to produce up to 12 new ones.

ABOVE Heathers (*Calluna*) are ideal for brightening up the garden through the second half of summer to the end of autumn. There's a choice of over 500 cultivars, and all need acid soil in a sunny site. The more extensive the spread, the more room you will need to stand back and enjoy it.

ABOVE The smaller rhododendrons can be replanted in an enlarged hole to create a batch of new young plants.

Plants for dropping

Berberis x stenophylla 'Irwinii'
Calluna
Cassiope
Daboecia cantabrica
Erica
Gaultheria
Kalmia angustifolia
Rhododendron, dwarf varieties
Vaccinium

The burying stage

This next stage involves digging up the old plant, with its roots intact, in early spring. Do not wait for the plant to start firing out new growth. Dig it up before that happens. Then roughly measure the distance from the bottom of the root ball to the top of the stems, but exclude the top 3.5cm (1½in) of growth. This top part will not be covered. Finally, fork up the bottom of the hole which will also facilitate good drainage and carefully drop the parent plant into the larger hole. Gently refill with crumbly, broken-up fine soil, firm down and water.

ABOVE The whortleberry (*Vaccinium corymbosum*) makes a large shrub, 1.5m (5ft) high and wide, with late spring white flowers.

DROPPING A HEATHER

1 Carefully fork a heather out of the ground when it is dormant, making sure that the roots are not damaged.

2 Go over the top growth with a pair of secateurs, nipping back any stems that are particularly congested or straggly.

3 Enlarge the hole so that when the plant is dropped back in only the top 3.5cm (1½in) remains visible above the soil.

4 Backfill with sand and garden compost or peat mixed in with the soil, and leave the stems to develop their own root systems.

Arranging the stems

If possible, arrange the stems poking up through the soil into a rough circle. This immediately makes clear what is valuable growth, and what are weeds, should any start bursting up through the soil around the plant. It is vital that all the weeds are promptly removed to avoid any competition from the vigorous, quick-growing plants.

The rooting stage

Over the next few months the buried stems will start rooting just below the soil surface. To ensure this happens, water the plant in dry spells over summer, keeping it well looked after. If there is a danger that you might accidentally start forking around the area, or that children might run over the buried plant, arrange a number of vertical canes around the plant and tie coloured string around them.

In autumn the plant will be ready for digging up. Carefully lift it out of the hole, and start cutting away the young growth, each with a batch of roots at the base. These plants can now go into a container or be planted out in the garden, where they need to be clearly labelled. The parent plant can be discarded.

Air layering

Propagating by air layering sounds tricky, but it isn't. Instead of bending growth down to the ground, often covering it with soil, all the action takes place on a stiff, upright stem. It was probably first practised in China 4,000 years ago, and is an excellent way of getting children interested in the art of propagation.

House plants

Air (or 'Chinese' or 'marcottage') layering is traditionally used to propagate a new plant from the top section of a house plant, especially when it has outgrown the available space, becoming much too tall.

Selecting a shoot

The key to success is selecting a young, not too woody stem, and then pinpointing a section about 25–30cm (10–12in) from the tip. There are then two possible ways of 'girdling' the stem. You can either use a clean, sharp knife to carefully remove a ring of bark 12mm (½in) wide, or use it to make an upward slicing cut into the bark. It needs to be about 2.5cm (1in) deep, going just less than halfway through the stem. Since this can quite tricky if you have not done it before, it might be worth trying this out on another not particularly productive stem.

ABOVE Camellias need acid soil, but if you cannot provide that, grow one in a tub specially filled with ericaceous compost (soil mix).

Plant support and rooting

If the stem is thin and weak, the length above the cut might bend right back and snap off. If that looks likely, tie a thin stick to the affected part to prevent any accidents.

The next stage involves applying a dab of rooting powder with a soft, clean paint brush around the cut surface. Then wedge a matchstick in the cut to keep it open.

Wetting the moss

You need a ball of sphagnum moss, available in all garden centres, which needs to be soaked in warm water for several hours to get it thoroughly moist. Then take it out and pack it

AIR LAYERING A MAGNOLIA

1 Use a very sharp thin-bladed knife to make an upward slice through the bark. Do this about 30cm (12in) from the tip.

2 Having dabbed rooting powder on the cut, keep the flap wedged open using a matchstick, but do not snap it off the stem.

3 Next, pack a ball of sphagnum moss which has been soaked and squeezed and opened into two halves, around the cut.

4 Wrap black polythene around the moss to keep it in position, and then tie or tape it up to make sure that it is completely airtight.

Plants for air layering

Likely contenders include:
Camellia
Cordyline fruticosa
Ficus elastica
Gardenia
Hamamelis
Hibiscus
Ilex
Magnolia
Schefflera

together, giving it a good squeeze, and use your two thumbs to open it out in two halves. They are then packed around the cut. While holding it, you will need another pair of hands to wrap a piece of black polythene around the moss, holding it in place.

Then tape up the overlap so that, in effect, the polythene forms an airtight bag. It is then held in place at the top and bottom using twist ties, but make sure you do not tie them so tightly that you are in danger of damaging the stem.

ABOVE *Magnolia* x *soulangeana* is a multi-stemmed shrub that flowers in the second half of spring when the new young foliage is just emerging. Even young plants that are three years old produce a very good show. It is one of the easiest magnolias to grow.

ABOVE A prolific berrying holly (*Ilex*), which adds bursts of bright colour to the winter garden and attracts large numbers of birds.

ABOVE Some of the more robust hibiscuses can be grown outside, but in cold climate areas they will need protection over winter.

Aftercare

Do not imagine that the plant now needs to be hot-housed to promote a good batch of roots. If anything, excess heat is damaging, so if the plant is in direct sun try wrapping a piece of aluminium foil around the polythene to give protection. Normal room temperature is fine. Occasionally, carefully unseal the polythene to make sure that the moss is still moist, and spray it if necessary. After several weeks (air layering indoors is obviously much quicker than outdoors, when it could take six months), when the roots have formed around the slice in the stem and started poking out through the moss, it is time to remove this section.

Removing the new plant

Make the cut just below the roots. You will then need to cut off the remaining length of stem on the parent plant, snipping it off just above a bud to help force out new growth. Remove the packaging – the polythene and aluminium, if used – and finally set the plant in a container filled with potting compost (soil mix). Do not try to remove the moss, because you might accidentally damage the roots.

Grafting

The use of grafting – taking two different plants and getting them to fuse together and function as one – is an excellent solution for those plants that cannot be easily propagated by other means, i.e. by seed or vegetative cuttings. The best way to see what a grafted plant looks like is by examining the base of a rose (and most garden roses are 'customized'), at the thick swelling at the bottom of the stem. This is the join (called the graft union), linking two different plants. The top growth (the scion) provides the big attractions, the colour and scent, and the bottom (the rootstock), the power and vigour, and often disease-resistance.

To graft two different plants, you need to master one basic surgical trick. Both sections must have their cambium (just beneath the bark, where the cells keep dividing, producing the essential new ones that cement the two sections together) exposed, and firmly bound together. Grafting is usually carried out when plants are dormant, through winter to early spring, or sometimes in midsummer. Ideally the scion will be dormant (not in leafy growth) with the rootstock just coming into growth. Get this right and the rest, in theory, is easy.

This chapter takes you through a wide range of techniques, starting off with the splice graft and then the whip and tongue, apical wedge grafting and side-veneer grafting, chip-budding and shield- or T-budding, and finally top grafting and approach grafting.

LEFT Almost every garden apple tree will have had its scion grafted on to a rootstock, which acts like an engine, providing all the power. It also determines the eventual size of the tree.

Splice, and whip and tongue grafting

There are several different kinds of grafting, and while they can be quite fiddly and tricky, some could not be easier. The best way to get started is by trying the splice graft.

Splice (or whip) grafting

An extremely simple graft, in which the two ends to be joined have the same diameter and a slanting cut, about 2.5cm (1in) long, so the one fits impeccably on top of the other. Use a sharp, sterilized knife so that each cut surface is smooth and flat, and then bind the two together immediately before they can dehydrate. Use grafting tape or alternatively a rubber band (though many gardeners still favour raffia or wax), and promptly remove it when the graft has callused over and healed. Always use a stable surface for cutting on, with good lighting, for this and the other techniques.

ABOVE Depending on which rootstock you choose, you can have the same variety of apple tree growing at a wide range of heights.

Benefits of grafting

Grafting is expensive, but most fruit trees are propagated this way for the following reasons:
• Grown on their own root systems, many would be excessively vigorous.
• Cultivars will not usually breed true from seed.
• A fruiting plant can be produced in a shorter period of time.
• Some weak-growing cultivars can be invigorated.

Whip and tongue grafting

For those good at carpentry, this is a very popular and effective way of propagating fruit trees and ornamentals, and is also a good alternative if a bud graft has not worked. Because the graft is made outdoors it is called field grafting. Instead of the two smooth, flat, joining surfaces of a splice graft, here each section has three exposed surfaces, and when joined they make a very effective bond.

Diameters

Again, note that the diameters of the scion and rootstock where the two join must be the same, up to 2.5cm (1in). Start by preparing the rootstock one year before, planting it where you want the tree to grow. Keep removing any side growth. When it is time to graft, in late winter or early spring, again remove any side growth and then cut off the top about 23cm (9in) above the soil. This must be a slanting, 3.5cm (1½in) long cut.

SPLICE GRAFTING

1 The stems of the rootstock and the scion must both be 12mm (½in) or less. Look for two matching plants to give an exact fit.

2 Make two slanting, matching cuts at the bottom of the scion and the top of the rootstock. The graft union must be an exact fit.

3 Finally, bind the two lengths together using grafting tape or raffia. You want a solid join without any wobble.

Trees for splice grafting

Acer palmatum	Pyrus
Hamamelis	Sorbus
Malus	Thuja
Picea	Wisteria

WHIP AND TONGUE GRAFTING

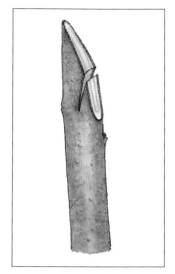

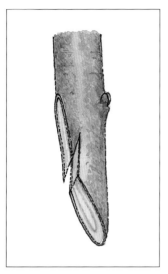

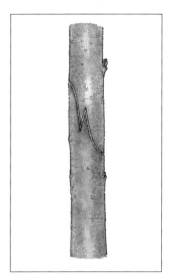

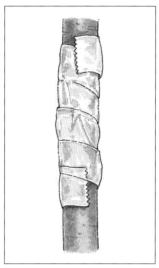

1 In late winter cut off the rootstock's top, 23cm (9in) above the soil. Make an upward-slanting cut 3.5cm (1½in) long. Then make a shallow incision one-third of the way up.

2 The bottom of the scion, which has three or four buds, needs a matching angled cut. Then make the shallow incision, so that the protruding tongue slips into the slot below.

3 Pair the two together. There needs to be complete contact of the exposed cambium wood, so carefully slice away any bumps to give an exact fit. This can be tricky, so take your time.

4 When the two lock together, they need to be firmly bound while the cambium surfaces gradually merge together. Use grafting tape. It can be removed after about eight weeks.

Scion

The scion needs to be a stout, strong, unblemished one-year-old shoot, about 23cm (9in) long, with three to four buds, the top one eventually becoming the leader. If collecting the scion before you are going to graft, keep it safe by planting it in the soil, leaving 6cm (2½in) exposed above ground. Make the top cut just above a bud, and the bottom, slanting cut 3.5cm (1½in) below a bud, and the same length and angle as the cut on the rootstock. But instead of firming the two together, as with the splice graft, do things differently. One-third of the way up the sloping cut on the rootstock make two short downward cuts, removing a narrow V-shaped wedge. Make a similar cut at the base of the scion, so that the two can firmly and perfectly lock together, and then bind them together with grafting tape. It will take about eight weeks before the tape can permanently be removed.

ABOVE Whip and tongue grafting is commonly applied to fruit trees, such as this plum, using hardwood shoots before new growth appears. The technique is also sometimes called field grafting for the simple reason that it is done outdoors. The best time is late winter or the start of spring.

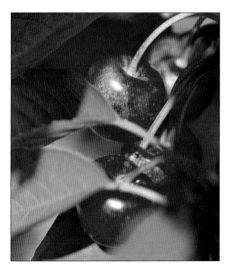

ABOVE When growing cherry trees, only prune in the growing season; if done when dormant, silver leaf disease might strike.

Apical wedge grafting

A technical name for what is essentially very simple, apical wedge grafting is used by commercial growers for woody ornamentals, including rhododendrons, witch hazel (*Hamamelis*) and crab apples (*Malus*), and climbers, giving good results.

The cut

Choose a strong, healthy scion that is pencil thick and one year old. Make the top cut just above a plump, fat bud (that will become the trunk) and the bottom cut below a bud. The final length should be about 15cm (6in). The bottom must now be cut into a pointed V shape that is 3.5cm (1½in) long. Next, the rootstock needs to be carefully lifted without damaging the roots. Then slice across the top of its stem – which needs the same diameter as the bottom of the scion – about 3.5cm (1½in) above the roots. Finally, make an inverted V in the centre of the stem so that the end of the scion can wedge perfectly into it. All four exposed cambium surfaces should have maximum contact.

ABOVE Most hibiscuses are tender shrubs, but if you live in a cold climate, use the sturdy, erect and hardy *H. syriacus* 'Diana', with its large white flowers and dark green leaves. It can be trained into a standard, and propagated by apical wedge grafting.

Bonding

Lock the scion and rootstock in place with grafting tape, and then pot up the plant in a container filled with potting compost (soil mix). The warmer the conditions in which it is now kept, the quicker the graft will take. Stand the container in a sheltered cold frame, greenhouse or gently heated propagator kept at 13°C (55°F), but do not go above 16°C (60°F). The tape can be removed when the graft has callused over in about six

ABOVE Beech makes excellent deciduous hedges, which can be clipped into various shapes. They like chalk or free-draining soil.

ABOVE The rowan tree (*Sorbus aucuparia*) makes a large 15m (50ft) tree with white spring flowers and reddish berries. Rowans are a marvellous source of striking clusters of aerial fruits, which are quickly taken by hungry birds with the onset of autumn.

weeks. Carefully peel off so that none is left. Thereafter keep nurturing it, watering as necessary, before planting out the following year. As with all forms of grafting, it is essential that you use a sharp, sterilized knife, and wash your hands before starting. Avoid touching and possibly infecting the exposed wood.

Saddle graft

A specialized variation on the apical wedge, it is worth understanding how evergreen rhododendrons (species and hybrids) might be tackled. Start by checking that the rootstock and scion have the same diameter, and are approximately pencil thick, but this time the cut is more of a rounded U than a sharp V-shape, with a matching concave U-shape at the bottom of the scion. Any large leaves should be cut in two horizontally to reduce moisture loss. When the graft union has finally taken, you can carefully remove the grafting tape.

ABOVE Propagate azaleas by apical wedge grafting, with the scion being wedged into the sliced-open top of the rootstock.

ABOVE Always buy a grafted wisteria, because those grown from seed can take up to 18 years, or even longer, to flower.

Trees, shrubs and climbers for apical wedge grafting

Actinidia	Cotoneaster	Malus (crab apple)	Rhododendron
Aesculus	Fagus	Parthenocissus	Rowan
hippocastanum	Hibiscus	Prunus, flowering	Wisteria

APICAL WEDGE GRAFTING

1 Use a healthy scion, nipping off the top above a bud, while slicing the base into a sharply angled V shape.

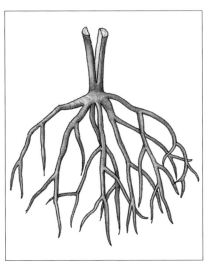

2 The V shape in step 1 now needs to be inserted into an upward-pointing V shape in the rootstock, with the same diameter as the scion. It is vital that there is an exact fit if the graft is to be successful.

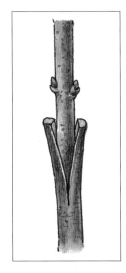

3 Now lock the two together, ensuring that the exposed cambium surfaces make full, excellent contact.

4 The join needs to be held firmly together using grafting tape, and the whole plant is potted up to promote new growth. Stand it in a bright, warm place, water as required and plant out the following year.

Side-veneer grafting

Used to propagate a wide range of fairly small plants, the specialized technique of side-veneer grafting is mainly applied to evergreen and deciduous trees and shrubs, including conifers that cannot be grown from seed and which are difficult to raise from cuttings. It differs from previous techniques in that the graft is made right at the side of the rootstock.

Rootstock

Carefully dig up the rootstock with a pencil-thick stem in late winter, when it is still dormant, and bring into a greenhouse for potting up. Unlike previous techniques it is not beheaded. Only give a gentle drink, but do provide some heat – no more than 16°C (60°F) – to generate extra root growth.

Scion

The strong, vigorous, one-year-old scion with a shoot at the top should have a base with a diameter matching, or possibly slightly less than, the

ABOVE Acers give a range of striking effects, from those with shedding, scrolling, papery bark to bold autumn colours before the leaves fall. Propagating acers can be tricky, with layering and side-veneer grafting two of the more popular methods.

rootstock. The base of the rootstock then has a sloping, downward, 2.5cm (1in) long cut made into it at an angle of 10 degrees, about 6cm (2½in) above ground. This upward-pointing flap needs to be removed at the base by making a horizontal cut no more than halfway in, forming

a shelf. The scion now needs to have its base stripped of any side growth, with a thin, 2.5cm (1in) long tongue cut to fit exactly against the slice taken out of the rootstock. The two are then firmly bound together with grafting tape or a rubber band, and are given a warm, humid environment at 13°C (55°F) in which to fuse together.

Matching growth rates

When selecting the scion, make sure that it comes from a plant that has a similar growth rate. If it suffers in comparison, or is much more vigorous than the rootstock, then there will be an imbalance, and in time the part with the poorer growth will be overtaken and overwhelmed.

Practice cuts

Making the thin slice in the rootstock at a downward sloping angle can be tricky, and it is worth having several practice attempts on other shoots before tackling it for real. Make sure that the cambium layer is clearly exposed.

ABOVE The optimum time for grafting conifers is late winter, when the roots are putting on growth but before new shoots appear.

ABOVE A white-stemmed birch (*Betula*), showing why they are so highly regarded, especially as the autumn leaves change colour.

ABOVE The one-species ginkgo (*G. biloba*) has existed for over 200 million years, and has been cultivated since 1754.

ABOVE *Picea pungens* 'Hoopsii' makes a small to medium-sized tree with a conical shape and striking bluish leaves.

ABOVE A sorbus, at its best in autumn mornings when the mists slowly lift and the red berries burst through the gloom.

Aftercare

Regular watering will not be necessary. Once the join has callused over after about eight weeks, remove the tape and nip back the top of the plant (i.e. the rootstock, not the grafted-on scion) in stages until it is level with the top of the graft. This will give a nicely shaped plant. Do not do this radically all in one go, because you will be removing the plant's photosynthetic, leafy, feeding factory. It can also come out of its warm, humid environment, gradually being given a cooler site with regular drinks.

SIDE-VENEER GRAFTING

1 The rootstock needs to have an angled, sloping cut sliced into it, just above soil level, with a horizontal shelf or base.

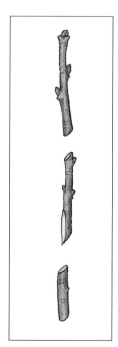

2 For the scion, remove a central section, leaving a sloping top cut and a shaved base.

3 Slip the base of the scion into the angled cut in the rootstock, and firmly bind the two together with tape.

Trees and shrubs for side-veneer grafting

Abies	Hamamelis
Acer	Larix
Betula	Magnolia
Cedrus	Malus
Daphne	Picea
Fagus	Pinus
Ginkgo	Robinia
Gleditsia	Sorbus

Side-wedge grafting

Similar to side-veneer grafting, side-wedge grafting differs in one key respect. Instead of making a very narrow shelf that the tongue at the end of the scion fits snugly against, the side-wedge has an upward-pointing flap in the rootstock into which the scion's tongue slips.

Chip-budding

A good example of a grafting technique practised by professionals when tackling fruit trees and various ornamentals, it has now become much more popular and widespread than T-budding because you can carry it out over a longer period, through the second half of summer – it has a high success rate.

Healthy growth

Start by selecting the most appropriate commercially available rootstock (which should be at least two years old), when dealing with fruit trees, and the scion from the current season's growth. Both should show strong, healthy growth, and the pencil-thick diameter of the rootstock stem should match that of the scion. In midsummer, remove all the growth from the bottom portion of the rootstock, flush to the stem, leaving a bare 30cm (12in) long leg.

The wedge

What you are looking for now is a fattening bud on the scion. Get rid of the soft end growth, and then the

Extension growth

If the new bud produces a flowering shoot, promptly get rid of the flower bud. You want the new section to put all its energy into developing valuable extension growth, creating a sound framework, not an attractive show. That comes later.

leaves, leaving stubs, and make the first cut 2cm (¾in) below a bud. It should angle up at 30 degrees, and only slice in to a depth of 5mm (¼in). The second cut starts 5cm (1½in) above the first one, and comes down at the same angle. In effect you are cutting out a triangular wedge with a bud and short, sliced-off leaf stalk. Take care not to damage it because this is going to be the new growth point that is inserted inside the rootstock.

Insertion

Locate the exact position where you want the bud to be inserted on the rootstock. Slice a wedge in the bark, just above a bud, and then carefully

ABOVE The advantage of a white-flowering hawthorn (*Crataegus*) is that it grows virtually anywhere, from cities to coasts.

slice up from beneath it so that the gap is exactly the same size and shape of the insertion.

The scion is then slotted in snugly so that the exposed lengths of cambium are in direct contact with each other. The insertion must be bound firmly in place with grafting tape, but make sure that

ABOVE The best laburnums are worth propagating for their shock of dangling yellow flowers as spring turns to summer.

ABOVE Both the scented and non-scented magnolias, grown for their lavish flowers, can be chip-budded to create extra numbers.

ABOVE The crab apple (*Malus*) makes an ornamental show with brightly coloured fruit, and will even fit into small gardens.

ABOVE Give pears a warm, sheltered spot, ideally against a sunny wall, and the fruit will juicily ripen through the autumn.

ABOVE An ornamental cherry tree, above a mass of daffodils, giving both spring blossom and later autumn leaf colours. Two of the best cherries include *Prunus serrula*, because of its shiny brown bark, and *P.* 'Shirotae', with its cloud-burst of flowers and fresh, apple-green foliage.

you do not tape over the bud or petiole. This stays on until the bud scion and rootstock have firmly joined, when the leaf stalk drops off. The bud also begins to swell, and this normally takes about eight weeks. The warmer the weather, the quicker the join.

The final cut

At the end of winter the rootstock is then cut back just above the new bud, provided it has taken successfully. Use an angled cut that will direct drops of rain and moisture away from this bud, to the opposite side, and not directly on to it. Keep an eye on the tree and get rid of any new growth emerging from below the bud when it starts exceeding 10cm (4in) long. If the bud did not take, the most likely reason is that the two exposed lengths of cambium were not in full contact. Get this right, and you should have a high success rate.

CHIP-BUDDING

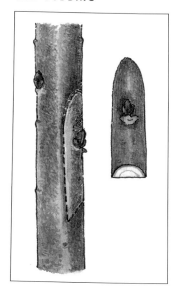

1 Remove a bud from the scion. Make a downward-angled cut below it, then cut down behind the bud from above.

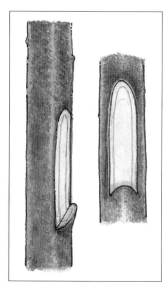

2 Make a matching cut to one side of the rootstock, cutting deep enough to expose the cambium layer beneath the bark.

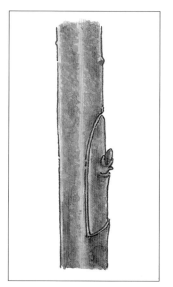

3 Slip the bud into the cut on the rootstock, making sure to line up the cambium layers. It should be a snug fit.

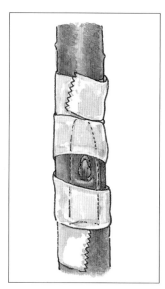

4 Wrap grafting tape around the rootstock to hold the bud in position, but take care to leave the growing point exposed.

Shield- or T-budding

An excellent technique for grafting roses and fruit trees. Though it can only be carried out when the bark of the rootstock is easily prized up, there is still a good time slot in late midsummer. Do not miss it.

Rootstock

Make sure that the rootstock (which should be two years old or more) is growing in the right place at least one year before making the graft. Its stem should be approximately pencil thick. Over a few weeks before starting work in early summer, to midsummer at the very latest, make sure that it is well watered whenever there is a dry spell. This is crucial to avoid hardening of the wood.

Scion bud

The bud that needs to be removed comes from this year's growth. Cut off a stem and then remove the foliage but leave 12mm (½in) of stalk, which you can use as a handle. You now need to carefully remove a mature bud (possibly halfway up the stem).

ABOVE Medlars need an open, sunny site, avoiding frost pockets that might ruin the spring blossom and potential crop. Do not pick the latter until it has been autumn-frosted.

About 12–18mm (½–¾in) below the bud, slice into the bark at an angle, so that you are going behind the bud (but not damaging it), then up, round and back so that the knife comes out well above the bud. In practice you will find that once the

knife has gone in, it is easier to lift up a strip of wood with the bud, and then cut it off, leaving a short tail. It should be a clean, simple extraction. Then turn over the bud and have a close look. If there is any woody tissue, scrape it away, especially when dealing with roses. (The worst case scenario is when the bud comes away with it, which means it is not mature and viable, so quickly look for a replacement.) Keep the bud fresh and safe in a moist plastic bag while making the next cut.

The T-cut

Next, strip off all the side growth up the bottom 30cm (12in) of the rootstock, and three-quarters of the way up this clean leg make a T-shaped cut in the bark. First make the 12mm (½in) wide horizontal cut, and then the vertical, 2.5cm (1in) cut. You need an old table knife or spatula to lift up the flaps and expose the cambium, whereupon the bud can be inserted just below the cross of the horizontal and vertical

ABOVE An unpruned apple tree on a spare patch of ground might not be as productive as an espalier, but it adds a carefree touch.

ABOVE Roses are easily propagated using shield-budding, but pull away any suckers from the parent the moment they appear.

cuts. If the bud will not fit exactly because there is a snag or tail of wood attached to it, slice it off flush with the horizontal cut. An exact fit is vital. Then secure it in place using grafting tape, but do not cover the bud itself. After about five weeks the scion and rootstock will have joined, and the tape is removed.

The final cut

Finally, cut back the rootstock in late winter, just above the new bud. Ensure that you make an angled cut to direct any moisture away from the shoot, down the opposite side of the rootstock. Also remove any growth emerging from below the new bud when it is more than 10cm (4in) long, and any flower buds on the new shoot. The aim is to produce good new extension growth.

Correct timing

Some gardening techniques are best done when you are in the right frame of mind but some, such as shield-budding, must be done at set times. Wait too long and you won't be able to lift the bark flaps for the new bud.

SHIELD-BUDDING

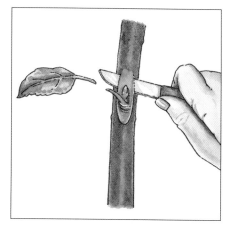

1 When removing the bud in early summer, leave a leaf stalk to act as a handle. Slice out the bud from below, going right behind it.

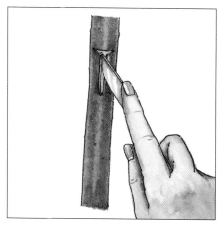

2 Then mark the insertion point in the rootstock, starting with the horizontal cut, and then make the vertical slice.

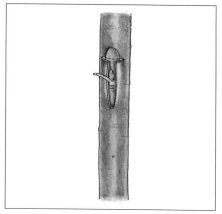

3 Lift the flaps to slide and wedge the bud in place. If there is a long wooden tail attached to it, slice it off to make a good fit.

4 Finally, tape the bud in place leaving the growing point free to emerge and develop. In late winter, cut back just above the bud.

ABOVE Once you've got a successful graft, plant damsons in soil with plenty of organic matter to help retain some extra moisture. The fresh fruit is very tart, so use it cooked to make jams and sauces.

ABOVE Peach trees are often best grown in a greenhouse, but it needs to be cool so that they can lie dormant over winter. For outside, use a midsummer-fruiting kind trained against a sunny, sheltered wall.

Top grafting

Sometimes it is necessary to change the cultivar of a mature apple tree, and possibly introduce a more effective pollinator, and the advantage of this technique is that the graft becomes productive quite quickly because it benefits from a well-established root system.

Cutting branches back

The first job seems quite brutal. All the branches are cut back (called 'dehorning') almost to the trunk, losing almost all of the top growth, in early spring before the big rush of sap. But do leave two of the less developed branches that will help pull up the sap, enabling the joins to take quickly. Use a sharp saw.

ABOVE Apple trees are ideal for top grafting, and those on a dwarfing rootstock can even be grown in a small garden.

ABOVE Having propagated a plum tree, add a thick spring mulch around the trunk to lock moisture in the ground and suppress weeds.

Taking the scions

You will need three or four dormant scions, with a final length of 10cm (4in), but tackle one at a time. When taking the first, make sure it has three nodes, and then slice a sliver off the bottom quarter, cutting down from just underneath a bud, leaving the bud below (on the opposite side) intact. The top of the scion has an angled cut, not pointing down on to the bud beneath but to the opposite side.

First insertion

Make a 2.5cm (1in) long slicing cut down from the edge of the sawn-off trunk, and then loosen the bark, carefully lifting it up. Prise it away with the side of a blunt old table knife but do not do this too vigorously and tear or splinter the bark. Provided you do this in early spring there should not be a problem. The aim is to expose the cambium. Then insert the first length of scion, checking that the exposed surface of the bottom of the sliced-off piece is in direct

ABOVE When propagating apple trees, make sure that the vigour of the rootstock is compatible with the size of your garden. M26 is one of the most popular rootstocks, giving an ultimate height of 2.4–3m (8–10ft). M27 and M9 give shorter growth, but both can be rather feeble.

ABOVE To give new, propagated quinces the best conditions, add an organic mulch to keep the roots cool and moist.

Final cuts

When the scions start growing – and they should make good progress powered by the established root system – look for the most vigorous. The next winter saw off the weakest scions, flush to the first cut when the trunk was sawn off, leaving just the most vigorous to grow away. Because these grafts are not the firmest, take care not to knock them. You might even find that they need a support, such as a cane tied firmly in place, as a temporary measure.

You can use top grafting on ornamental trees, but it does tend to change their shape, so think twice before trying this technique. With fruit trees it does not matter.

ABOVE Give crab apples a prominent position in full sun, because the brightly coloured fruits make a strong visual feature.

contact with the rootstock's cambium. Continue working around the sawn-off trunk, adding the other scions at regular intervals. When the final one is in position, wrap grafting tape firmly around the end of the sawn-off trunk, locking all the scions in place. Also carefully seal the exposed, raw end of the trunk with grafting wax or grafting paint to keep it waterproof and prevent it drying out. The tape should be ready to come off after five to eight weeks.

The cleft variation

You can alternatively make a cleft or cut across the top of the sawn-off stem, about 2.5cm (1in) deep, and then insert two scions in that, one at either end. Make the cut using a wedge and mallet. The cut will be sufficiently springy to close up tightly, holding the scions in place. You will then need to paint over the top of the sawn-off stem with grafting wax or paint in order to exclude moisture and eliminate drying, and eventually remove the weaker of the two scions.

TOP GRAFTING

1 You need to make three clean, slicing vertical cuts in the bark, about 2.5cm (1in) long, an equal distance apart.

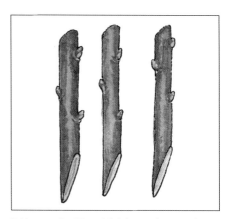

2 Line up the 10cm (4in) long scions, each with three buds and angled cuts on the bottom and top.

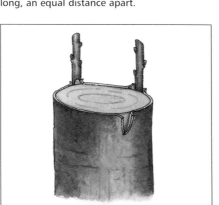

3 Insert each scion. Wedge the bottom end into the cut, with the angled cut making full contact with the cambium. Slide right down.

4 Tape the scions in place and then seal the end of the branch with grafting wax or paint. Eventually remove the weakest two scions.

Approach grafting and grafting tips

If you get hold of an old propagators' handbook, you will find all kinds of highly specialized grafting methods, many that are no longer used or taught. But some are good fun and worth knowing about, and are definitely worth a try.

Appproach grafting

This technique can be used to propagate a particularly important dying tree, and anything else that is proving tricky by other methods, including pot plants. In the case of the latter, start by standing the two plants next to each other, and look for two stems that easily touch. Both should be this year's growth. It is very important that you do not try and force them together in case they snap or get damaged. Then carefully slice off a 3.5cm (1½in) long strip of the outer bark on one to expose the cambium, and then do exactly the same to the other, checking that they are going to be in full contact. Next, bind the two exposed areas together with grafting tape.

ABOVE Hollies can be propagated in various ways, one of the simplest being an approach graft, in which two plants, one with an established root system, are conjoined.

Continued growth

While the two cambiums join, both plants carry on growing and there is no danger that either will dry out. When the join has taken, after 10 weeks or so, remove the tape and make two cuts. First, remove the top of the rootstock, just above where the two plants now join. Then sever the scion just below where the two join, retaining the leg and roots of one plant, and the top growth of the other. Keep the soil around the rootstock well watered during dry spells in the growing season so that the new plant is not stressed. Add a thick mulch after a night of heavy rain to lock moisture in the ground.

APPROACH GRAFTING

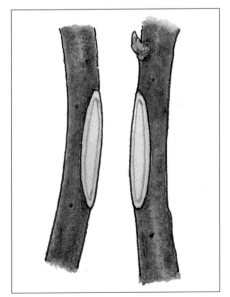

1 When standing two pot plants side by side, select two facing stems. Slice off 3.5cm (1½in) strips to expose the cambium.

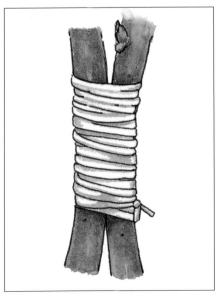

2 Gently bring them together, so that the exposed lengths are in full contact, and then bind together with grafting tape.

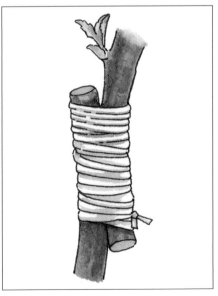

3 After about 10 weeks, remove the head of the rootstock plant above the tape, and the bottom of the scion plant below it.

Grafting tips

Infection

Make sure that you always use sharp, sterilized equipment. Anything that touches the exposed cambium can theoretically pass on an infection. Given how much skill, care, effort and time can go into making a successful graft, it is ridiculous to ruin everything when just a few minutes at the start, and throughout the operation, can eliminate a potential hazard.

Scions and rootstock

It is important that scions are healthy and vigorous. Do not perpetuate any problems. That equally applies to the rootstock, which must be virus-free. Both sections must also be compatible.

Vigilance

Do not let new growth appear on the rootstock below the scion. You want to channel the plant's energy into making the new bud take and then grow away strongly, without it being diverted to other shoots.

Full contact

The key to success is making sure that the exposed cambium on the scion and on the rootstock are locked together firmly, before being taped in place. If there is a gap between the two, they cannot join together. And when you have made the two cuts, act quickly or the wood will dry out.

Forced wait

If you are taking large quantities of scions before it is time to make the implants, you can keep them in good shape by tying them together in bundles, with the bottoms together. Label the batch, noting the cultivar and the date taken. Plant the bundle in the soil, leaving 6cm (2½in) exposed above ground.

RIGHT When propagating, it is sometimes easy to forget that you might be creating magnificent giants such as these conifers.

Pests and diseases

The best way of growing problem-free plants is to start with healthy, vigorous forms, and to grow them well. That means starting with fresh compost (soil mix) and fresh seed, which will have a better germination rate than old seed, and using equipment (seed trays and pots, etc.) that has been freshly sterilized or scrubbed, even if it was thoroughly cleaned before being stored away.

Healthy young plants stand a much better chance of fighting off problems than poor, weak ones, and problems can pile up in the protected environment of a greenhouse. Beware the following.

• Poor ventilation – note that greenhouse doors and windows, and lids of cold frames, should be propped open whenever possible, even in winter.

• General clutter – put away all pots and containers etc., so that pests (including mice) will not have good access to hiding places, and fungal spores cannot build up. Keep on top of the mess.

• High temperatures – especially when they are with poor and high light levels.

• Poor-draining compost (soil mix) – you do not want seedlings and cuttings sitting (and rotting) in soggy conditions when they are dormant.

• Overfeeding – resulting in leggy, sappy growth that is a prime target for sap-sucking creatures and various diseases.

• Also note – biological controls cannot be used in conjunction with insecticides.

PESTS

Aphids Also called blackfly and greenfly – though they come in other colours, including pink, orange, yellow, brown and white these are tiny sap-feeding insects, 1–6mm long. All suck the sap of a plant. Strongly growing plants will often shrug them off with only minor and temporary damage, but with small, delicate specimens the aphids can seriously weaken them and distort the shoot tips and new foliage. They can also spread viruses, so be extra careful with plants that are prone to viral disease. Look for the excreted sticky substance – called honeydew – on the upper leaf surface, that falls from the leaves above, attracting sooty mould. Badly infested plants should be destroyed. Control by picking off small numbers and crushing them, by applying a jet of water from a hose, and by using organic and chemical sprays. The parasitic wasp *Aphidias matricariae* works above temperatures of 18°C (64°F).

Bird and cats The former tuck into seedlings, basically a tasty salad, especially early in the morning when they strut round the garden hauling out what they like. Scarecrows do not scare crows, let alone anything else. Canes with string running from one to another with old CDs might help. Netting is the best bet, but make sure it is tightly pinned down at the sides because birds can get in and get trapped – and if a cat gets in, the seedlings will get shredded in the mayhem.

Aphids

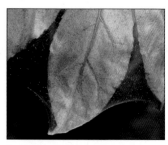
Red spider mites

Scale insects

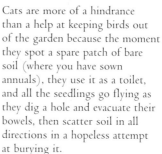
Sciarid fly

Cats are more of a hindrance than a help at keeping birds out of the garden because the moment they spot a spare patch of bare soil (where you have sown annuals), they use it as a toilet, and all the seedlings go flying as they dig a hole and evacuate their bowels, then scatter soil in all directions in a hopeless attempt at burying it.

Caterpillars The larval stage of moths and butterflies feed on roots, stems, flowers, fruit and seedpods, with the cabbage white butterfly, elephant hawk moth and winter moth quickly shredding leaves. They also attack seedlings in autumn. They hide during the day under pots and in piles of dead leaves. Small numbers can easily be removed by hand, but use the biological control *Bacillus thuringiensis* or a systemic insecticide against large infestations.

Red spider mites Infestations occur in hot, dry conditions outside or more typically in the greenhouse or on a sunny windowsill. The mites are minuscule, eight-legged sap-suckers, initially yellowish-green but turning orange-red in autumn. They multiply at a fast rate, and can be seen with a magnifying glass moving from stem to leaf on fine webbing. Hang perforated envelopes containing the predatory mite *Phytoseiulus*

persimilis that attacks the pest. Alternatively use a systemic insecticide and/or grow plants in a humid atmosphere, giving repeated sprayings of water.

Scale insects When you see a cluster of immobile brown bumps or flattish discs on stems and leaves, plants are being attacked by sap-sucking insects with a shell-like covering over their bodies. Some excrete a sticky substance called honeydew on the leaves, leading to sooty moulds. The problem can occur all year on indoor plants, or in midsummer outside. Heavy infestations limit plant growth and make the leaves turn yellow. Control by using the parasitic wasp *Metaphycus helvolus* in a greenhouse, or a systemic spray.

Sciarid fly Also called fungus gnats, these tiny black flies congregate on the surface of the compost (soil mix) in pots. The larvae live in the soil – and they are especially fond of peat – where they feed on roots and organic detritus, and consequently seedlings and cuttings put on poor, limited growth. Established plants rarely suffer, and the flies are more of an annoyance to humans than the plants. The best way to prevent an attack is to use free-draining, sterilized compost, and to make sure that it is never overwatered. Cover the compost surface with a 5mm (¼in) deep

Blackbird

Caterpillar from vapourer moth

Slug

Snail

Vine weevil

Whitefly

layer of grit. Once you see the flies running across the soil surface and around the rim of the pot, use an insecticide or hang up sticky yellow strips so that they are near soil level. The predatory mite *Hypoaspis miles* feeds on the maggots of various pests in the soil.

Slugs and snails It is rare to have a garden without slugs and snails, but you can try to limit their damage. They will quickly demolish stems and seedlings, attacking dahlias and lilies, for example. (All slugs were once snails but have lost their shells, replacing them with mucus, and the reason why one gaily slithers along in the wake of another's goo is that it does not have to make its own supply.) The best predators are hedgehogs, frogs and thrushes, so surround the garden with a wild area for the former, and site ponds among the more formal flowery areas. Keep going out at night to pick them off by hand (what happens next depends on how squeamish you are, with drowning a fairly quick death sentence). Also try any of the countless deterrents, from saucers of beer sunk in the ground (more drowning) to surrounding prize plants with sharp sand. Nematodes can be watered into beds and borders to seek out and destroy slugs (snails

being largely immune). Pots can be wrapped round with copper tape, and some toxic slug pellets are efficient killers, but check whether they are hazardous to other creatures, killing the very predators you want to encourage.

Vine weevils A potential killer of established pot plants (rarely those growing out in the open, and rarely seedlings and cuttings), with the adults being less of a pest than the larvae. But when you spot the adults (they cut semicircular sections out of the edges of leaves) act quickly. They are 9mm (3/8in) long, dull black beetles usually seen at night (hiding during the day) scuttling about the foliage, which they feed on. They lay their tiny, almost impossible-to-see eggs in the soil (that is 1,500 eggs in a female's lifespan) and the emerging fat, white, legless, C-shaped grubs have beige heads. They devour a plant's roots and suddenly you've got a dead plant that was happy and thriving the day before. The grubs are also quite capable of boring into tubers. Check pot plants at night looking for the adults, and anywhere they might hide (e.g. in upturned pots), and use imidacloprid spray on the leaves. Water parastic nematodes (*Heterorhabditis*) into the compost when the soil temperature is over 55°C (13°F) and the surface is

moist. Encourage ground beetles that prey on the larvae.
Whiteflies Keep checking under leaves for colonies of 2mm (1/8in)-long, white, winged insects on greenhouse plants, e.g. tomatoes and cucumbers. They take off and swarm at the slightest touch. The flies live just three weeks and breed quickly, with both young and adults sucking the sap. Like other insects they can also excrete sticky honeydew on the leaves. The upshot is that plants perform badly, and might be infected by a virus. Growing the strong-smelling French marigolds (*Tagetes patula*) nearby is a proven deterrent, but you can also use sticky yellow traps hanging on plants, the parasitic wasp *Encarsia formosa* – which will not eradicate a big infestation, but will severely reduce it provided night temperatures stay above 10°C (50°F) with the day ones above 18°C (64°F) – or a systemic insecticide.

DISEASES
Botrytis The commonest fungal problem, immediately recognized by the fuzzy, greyish mould appearing on flowers, stems and leaves. The spores rapidly spread. To discourage an attack, cut off any injured or dead parts of the plant and promptly discard.

Damping off A fungal disease that attacks germinating seeds and also rots seedlings at soil level. Avoid high humidity, and space out the seedlings, giving them room to grow uncluttered.
Mildew There are a wide range of mildews, most attacking a particular host plant, and all have the same symptoms. They include a dry coating of white powder on the flowers, shoot tips and/or leaves in summer, causing stunted growth and poor flowering. Dry soil and humid, stagnant air encourage the disease. Affected new foliage should be promptly removed or sprayed with a fungicide.
Rust Typically seen on roses, patches of bright orange appear on the underside of the foliage, with yellow on the top side, in bad cases resulting in heavy defoliation. It is absolutely vital that you promptly collect every last leaf because the spores can persist on fallen infected leaves on the ground over winter. Avoid by ensuring plants have an open centre, pruning to an outward-facing bud, and good air circulation. Spray with mancozeb.
Viruses The wide range of viruses are usually caused by aphids or infected tools, and can result in mottling and stunting. Sterilize tools and burn infected plants, and do not propagate from them.

Botrytis

Mildew

Rust

Cucumber mosaic virus

Glossary

Annual Plant that goes through its entire life cycle – germinating, flowering and setting seed – within a growing season.

Anther The part of the stamen where the pollen forms.

Basal cuttings Cuttings taken from the bottom of a plant.

Basal plate The bottom of a bulb from which new bulbs can grow.

Bedding plant An annual, biennial or perennial that is used to make a temporary display in a bed or border. The advantage is that new displays keep being created using a different mixture of plants.

Biennial plant Taking two years to complete their entire life cycle, with growth occurring in the first year, flowering and setting seed in the second.

Biological control Using living organisms – including the wasp (*Encarsia formosa*) and predatory mite (*Phytoseiulus persimilis*) – to control pests and diseases.

Bisexual Flowers with both male and female reproductive parts (hermaphrodite).

Bog garden Area of waterlogged soil – that does not dry out in summer – for plants that grow in the wild in such conditions. If the garden does not have such an area, it can be created by siting it next to a pond where the water is made to seep from the latter to the former, or using pond liner with holes pierced in it, buried under the ground.

Bolting Producing flowers and seed prematurely.

Bottom heat Artificial heat applied via electric cabling under the compost (soil mix)

Annual (*Dianthus* 'Mrs Sinkins')

Biennial (*Oenothera biennis*)

Ericaceous (*Rhododendron* 'Brilliant Blue')

to stimulate seed germination or rooting, in a greenhouse, to get quicker results than will occur in the colder conditions outside.

Bract A modified leaf that emerges at the base of a flower and, when large and brightly coloured, is often confused with the actual flower.

Budding The means of propagation in which the bud of one plant is grafted on to another plant.

Cold frame Outside glass-covered garden frame, without artificial heat, used for germinating seeds and getting seedlings and larger plants to acclimatize to outdoor conditions.

Compost Organic matter that has been gathered together and kept while it decomposes, being eventually used as a mulch.

Cotyledons The first set of leaves on a germinated seed, and which are invariably different from the second (true) set.

Crown That part of a plant that sits on, or just above, soil level, and from which new stems appear.

Cultivar A cultivated variety that first occurred naturally or through breeding.

Cutting That part of a plant – whether root, leaf, or shoot – that has been removed at various stages of growth and used to create a brand new plant.

Deciduous A plant that sheds or loses its foliage at the end of the growing season.

Dioecious Indicates that the male and female parts occur on separate plants. Usually mentioned when you need to buy a male and female to produce fruit.

Dormant The period when a plant rests before breaking into growth as more favourable growing conditions emerge.

Ericaceous Those plants requiring acid soil if they are to thrive. Typical examples include camellias, heathers and rhododendrons.

Etiolated Feeble, spindly, over-long, often bleached growth occurring in poor light.

Evergreen A plant that retains its leaves through more than one growing season. Most shed and replace their leaves throughout the year, rather than all in one season.

Frost hardy Plants that can survive temperatures to -5°C (41°F).

Frost tender Plants that should not be exposed to temperatures that dip below 5°C (41°F).

Fully hardy Plants that can stay outside all year because they can survive at -15°C (5°F).

Germination The process by which a seed evolves into a young plant, so that it has both roots and shoots.

Graft When the shoot of one plant is permanently attached and secured to the rootstock of another so that the two grow together and function as one.

Ground cover Typically low-growing plants that are valued because they spread across the soil surface and block out weeds.

Hardening off Plants that have been raised in a protected, artificial environment being exposed to conditions closer to those outdoors before going permanently outside.

Heel cutting A cutting with a sliver of bark or wood attached that minimizes the possibility of rot.

Insecticide Chemical used to kill unwanted insects.

Internode The length of stem lying between two nodes.

Frost hardy (*Alyssum spinosum* 'Roseum')

Frost tender (*Impatiens walleriana*)

Fully hardy (*Anemone blanda*)

John Innes This is not a brand name but a recipe for potting composts (soil mixes), with the different numbers (1 to 3) denoting the relative fertilizer strength with No. 3, the strongest, being used on long-term, greedy plants (shrubs). Seedlings can only take in small amounts of nutrients and would be damaged by higher concentrations.

Lateral Growing from the side.

Layering When a stem is used to create a new plant. It needs to be bent down to, and kept in contact with, the soil so that it has a chance to root. When the roots have formed the stem can be severed from the parent and used as an independent plant.

Leaf axil The angle between the stem and the leaf or its stalk.

Leaf cutting Using a leaf, or a portion of a leaf, to propagate new plants.

Leaf mould Extremely useful dark brown, friable, organic substance made from rotted, decayed leaves that is high in humus but low in nutrients. Used as a mulch and soil conditioner. It occurs naturally in woodlands where the ground is covered in fallen, rotting leaves – but note that it is illegal to collect it from the wild.

Microclimate The local climate within a specific area (or part of a garden) that is different from the conditions elsewhere, for example caused by sheltering walls providing greater protection than elsewhere in the landscape.

Monoecious Each individual plant has both male and female flowers.

Mulch

Mound layering Piling earth up around an established plant so that when the stems are kept in contact with the soil (as in layering) they start to root. The rooted stems can be cut from the parent plant and used as new plants. Very useful technique where lots of new plants are required.

Mulch A layer of organic or inorganic material placed on the ground, typically around plants, for several reasons. It protects the roots in cold winters, it helps keep moisture locked in the ground so that it does not quickly evaporate, and organic types improve the soil structure and feed plants as worms drag it underground.

Node The point at which shoots or leaves emerge from a stem.

Offset A small, young plant that naturally (and vegetatively) occurs, being attached (and easily separated from) the parent. Most commonly seen on bulbs and other plants with rosettes of growth (such as *Sempervivums*).

Petiole A leaf stalk.

pH The measure of a soil's acidity or alkalinity.

Photosynthesis The essential process by which a plant absorbs the energy from sunlight using chlorophyll, with carbon dioxide and water being converted into sugars and oxygen.

Pinching out Removing the growing tip of a (usually) young plant, activating replacement buds further down, thereby giving a bushier and/or more floriferous plant.

Offset (*Sempervivum tectorum*)

Pollination When pollen is transferred by various means (including insects, animals, wind, etc.) from the male anther to the female stigma.

Potting on When a plant's root system is too large for its current container and it needs to be moved into a larger one, giving room for further growth.

Potting up Inserting a seedling or cutting into a pot filled with compost (soil mix).

Pricking out Transferring a seedling or young cutting from its first container into a slightly larger one, giving it more room to grow.

Rhizome An underground or soil-level, usually horizontal, fleshy storage organ producing both roots and top growth.

Rootstock A plant used in a graft to provide the roots.

Runner The colloquial name for a spreading, underground shoot that bears new growth.

Pollination

Scion A plant used to provide the top growth to be joined to the rootstock.

Sport A shoot that shows a different characteristic (e.g. colour) from the rest of the plant. It can be propagated by taking cuttings.

Sucker A shoot that appears from the underground part of a plant, typically the roots. When it has rooted, it can be severed from the parent and used as a new plant unless it comes from the rootstock of a grafted plant, in which case it is best discarded because it will not resemble the attractive top growth, even though it might be extremely vigorous.

Tuber An underground storage organ formed from the roots or stem.

Union The point at which the rootstock and scion join together.

Variegation The often irregular arrangement of pigments on a leaf, usually caused by a mutation or even disease.

Rhizome (*Agapanthus* 'Loch Hope')

Scion (quince)

Tuber (*Dahlia* 'Fascination')

Index

Page numbers in *italics* refer to the illustrations.

Butomus umbellatus

Convallaria majalis

Eupatorium purpureum

Fuchsia 'Swingtime'

Lilium longiflorum

AUTHOR'S ACKNOWLEDGEMENTS
With thanks to the Dowager E. de Pauley, Alexander, Barney, the directors and staff at RBA productions, and especially the very talented, upbeat editor Felicity Forster who knocked this massive enterprise into shape and skilfully made everything happen.

PUBLISHER'S ACKNOWLEDGEMENTS
George Drye, estate manager, kindly provided plant material and allowed us to shoot in the gardens and glasshouses at Lamport Hall (www.lamporthall.co.uk).

Thank you to Angus and Jo Lock, Ian and Wendy Hall, Tony and Anne White, and Jim Butlin, who also provided plants from their gardens.

Philippa Anderson of Haxnicks (www.haxnicks.co.uk) supplied many of the tools and equipment used in the photographs.

The publisher would also like to thank the following for allowing their photographs to be reproduced in the book (t=top, b=bottom, l=left, r=right, m=middle).
Felicity Forster: 50bl, 61bl, 61bm, 61br. iStockphoto: 25tr, 28br, 29bl, 29bm, 119tl. Photolibrary: 26tr, 27br, 29br, 37t, 43bm, 57b, 60t, 61m, 85b, 97bl, 101tr.

Onopordum acanthium